COLLECTOR'S GUIDE TO BUBBLE BATH CONTAINERS

IDENTIFICATION & VALUES

GREG MOORE
and
JOE PIZZO

COLLECTOR BOOKS

A Division of Schroeder Publishing Co., Inc.

The current values in this book should be used only as a guide. They are not intended to set prices, which vary from one section of the country to another. Auction prices as well as dealer prices vary greatly and are affected by condition as well as demand. Neither the Authors nor the Publisher assumes responsibility for any losses that might be incurred as a result of consulting this guide.

Searching for a Publisher?

We are always looking for knowledgeable people considered to be experts within their fields. If you feel that there is a real need for a book on your collectible subject and have a large comprehensive collection, contact Collector Books.

On the front cover:

Bullwinkle, R – 3, $45.00 – 50.00; Woodsy Owl, R – 4, $60.00 – 70.00;
Creature from the Black Lagoon, R – 3, $100.00 – 120.00; Mighty Mouse, R – 4, $45.00 – 50.00;
Batman, R – 1, $5.00 – 10.00; R2-D2 (Star Wars), R – 2, $15.00 – 20.00;
Mickey Mouse, R – 2, $20.00 – 25.00; My Little Pony, R – 3, $15.00 – 20.00;
Cecil the Sea Serpent (Beany and Cecil), R – 3, $20.00 – 25.00

Cover design:
Beth Summers

Book design:
Michelle Dowling

~ ~

COLLECTOR BOOKS
P.O. Box 3009
Paducah, Kentucky 42002–3009

Copyright © 1999 by Greg Moore and Joe Pizzo
Printed in the United States by Image Graphics Inc. Pacucah, KY

~ ~

CONTENTS

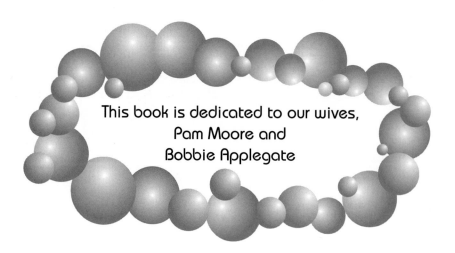

This book is dedicated to our wives,
Pam Moore and
Bobbie Applegate

ACKNOWLEDGMENTS

Joe Pizzo wishes to thank John and Jana Fulbright for their photography; Barbara and Barbara Dunsford of Great Britain for acquiring British bubble bath containers — Soapies, as they call them; and Joe and Margaret Rasnick who always return from their flea market excursions with a bubble bath bottle that Joe needs.

Greg Moore wishes to acknowledge the contributions of Pete Nowicki, Jon Deming, Steve West, and Bill Keats.

Both authors are particularly indebted to Matt and Lisa Adams who not only found many key bottles for us, but also shared their expertise in the production of this book.

Both authors would also like to thank Kevin Moore for keeping us up to date on Canadian bottles.

Thanks go out to Larry Parsel and the crew at 3L Printing for developing the prospectus for this project.

We also appreciate the information that we have received from Norman Auslander of Lander Co. and Julie Beno of Minnetonka Brands.

And finally, we want to thank all those many individuals who have helped us build our collections over the years.

INTRODUCTION

There once was a time when children everywhere hated washing their hair and taking a bath. That was before companies such as Purex and Colgate-Palmolive took a cue from the cereal makers, who had made an art of enticing children to ask for their product. The hook was simple: put a prize in the box.

Beginning in the 1960s, the soap manufacturers went one better. Instead of placing a prize in a bottle of bubble bath or shampoo, they made the bottle itself the prize and the character-shaped soap container was "born." Children eagerly took their bubble baths and had a toy when the bottle was empty.

The first of these bottles to be produced for a mass market were most likely the charming Betty Bubbles (Figure 1) and her comic counterpart, Bobo Bubbles (Figure 2). Both of these were distributed by the Lander Company starting in the mid-1950s. While Purex and Colgate-Palmolive may not have been the first to put their soap in a character-shaped bottle, their Bubble Clubs and Soakies are the best known and most popular with collectors. (In fact, the name Soaky has become synonymous with character-shaped soap container.)

Fig. 2

The Purex bottles, many of which were titled Bubble Club and featured Hanna Barbera characters almost exclusively, were produced through the 1960s and into the 1970s. (In the later years, the bottles are sometimes found labeled under the name of Purex spin-offs or subsidiaries such as Roclar, Milvern, or Clark.) The bubble bath itself came in either liquid or powder form. The liquid soap came in a bottle which had a screw-off cap under the removable head of the character, while the powder came in two versions: a single unit bottle with a plugged opening in the bottom; or a bottle with a removable head, under which there was a plug in the neck. There were four characters made in this latter style: Huckleberry Hound, Baba Looey, Quick Draw McGraw, and Yogi Bear. A slot was cut in their hats so they could serve as a bank when the bottle was empty. Many people find these bottles empty and assume they were simply banks. However, they have all been found with tags (Figure 3) which clearly indicate that they originally contained powdered bubble bath.

Soakies were produced by Colgate-Palmolive in the mid-1960s and featured characters from a variety of stables, such as Walt Disney Produc-

Fig. 1

Fig. 3

tions, Warner Brothers Pictures, P.A.T. Ward Productions, King Features Syndicate, and others. Soaky was a liquid bubble bath that came in three distinctly different types of bottles. The earlier Soaky bottles had the cap on top of the character's head. Some, like Bugs Bunny and

Fig. 4

Deputy Dog were cleverly embellished with ears or a cowboy hat over the cap.

Another variety of Soaky featured a bottle with the cap under the character's head (or torso in the case of Snow White and Cinderella).

A later version, called the Soaky Squeezables, must have been created to satisfy the need for instant gratification. The toy was a soft rubber figure which slipped over a plain cylindrical bottle of liquid soap (Figure 4). The child could have the toy before the first bath was ever taken.

Compared to the 1960s and early 1970s the period from the late 1970s through the 1980s was marked by a paucity of character-shaped soap containers. A notable exception was the set of eight Star Wars character bottles produced by Omni in the early 1980s, in both a bubble bath and a shampoo variation. Other companies such as Lander, Cosrich, and DuCair Bioescence (later to become Kid Care) managed to keep an occasional supply of comic character bottles on the shelves during this period.

The 1990s have seen a resurgence in the issuing of these bottles, which are becoming more and more elaborate. Lately, Cosrich and KidCare have been churning out bottles in the shape of our favorite movie and cartoon characters for distribution during the holiday season. In 1994, the Canadian company, Centura, issued nine bottles illustrating Mickey and Minnie Mouse through the years in connection with Mickey's 65th anniversary. Minnetonka Brands created minor works of art with their Warner Brothers character bottles issued for Christmas 1996. Warner Brothers stores themselves are getting into the act, using the name Soakies for the Marvin Martian, Bugs Bunny, and Sylvester/Tweety bottles issued in 1996. And in addition, an abundance of beautifully detailed bottles are now being produced in England and Italy.

The field of collecting character bubble bath containers is one that is wide open and ever growing. While it is a challenge to find that elusive bottle at a reasonable rate before another collector does, there are still enough bottles out there that even a novice can build an impressive collection with a modest investment.

HOW TO USE THIS BOOK
I. Organization
The authors were faced with the dilemma of how to organize this book. We could possibly

have gone chronologically or by maker or alphabetically by character.

We finally decided it would be more fun to bring characters together by genre. There are 13 chapters, each representing a collection of characters that bear some commonality such as space and science fiction, heroes and super heroes, or Hanna Barbera characters, etc. There will necessarily be some overlap of categories (for example, should the Avon Batmobile soap bottle go with Avons, super heroes, or vehicles?) and we made judgment calls as to which category takes precedence. If you are unsure as to where to find your favorite character, consult the index in the back of the book.

II. The Descriptive Text

Under each photograph there is a uniform descriptive text, which lists:

a.) the name of the character (with any possible variations)
b.) the distributor (when known)
c.) the country of origin if different than the USA
d.) the date of issue (when known)
e.) the rarity of the item (R - #) on a scale of 1 to 5
f.) the estimated value

Some explanation of items (e) and (f) are in order and are given on the next pages.

THE RARITY SCALE

R 1 indicates a very common bottle, most likely very recent and still available in retail stores within the last few years.

R 2 indicates an item that is somewhat common. While such items may not be available in retail stores, they come up frequently at auctions and can be found easily enough in flea markets or even garage sales.

R 3 indicates an item that is not very common. Items in this category usually show up in antique malls or toy shows and occasionally come up at auctions. They can also be found by checking the ads in toy publications. (This category is also used for most of the recent items from outside North America. Even though the item is common in the country of origin, it is not very common in America.)

R 4 indicates an item that is relatively rare. One has to hunt diligently or offer top dollar to unearth an item in this category, but perseverance will always prevail.

R 5 indicates an extremely rare item. Many collectors may hunt for years and not find a particular item in this category.

ESTIMATED VALUES

The single most important consideration of this book is that the price ranges that have been assigned to bottles cataloged should serve only as a guideline to approximate values. You will find that some items classified as rare are listed in a low price range and other items that are not very rare command high prices. This illustrates the demand side of supply and demand.

The ultimate value of any item is what someone is willing to pay. This pricing guide lists approximate values as per the current market prices obtained from auctions, toy shows, trade periodicals, and the authors' experiences from years of collecting and interacting with other collectors.

Price ranges apply to a bottle that would rate at least a 9 (on a scale of 10) as far as condition is concerned. Paint scuffs and minor cracks can reduce the value by a significant amount. Excessive paint wear and major cracks can render a bottle valueless to a collector. The prices quoted in this book do not reflect the existence of the original box, wrapper, label, or tag. These original paper items can increase the value of older bottles by up to 50%.

This book, which catalogs character-shaped soap bottles from the 1950s to the present is as current, accurate, and comprehensive as is believed possible. As accurately as we have tried to describe the values, the authors and this publication cannot be responsible for any financial losses that occur through the use of this book. Prices will always fluctuate as certain characters become more or less popular and other market factors come into play. The Law of Collecting says that you will always see an item offered at less than you just paid — and in better condition. The Law of Selling says that you will always find a buyer willing to pay more than you have asked — after you have already sold the item. If you sell an item for more than a listed price or buy an item for less than a listed price, consider yourself lucky. Enjoy this hobby and only pay what an item is worth to enhance your enjoyment of your collection.

PROTECTING YOUR COLLECTION

Most character soap bottles, particularly the older ones, are made of hard plastic which becomes brittle with age and has a tendency to crack very easily. The cracking usually occurs either when container is dropped or when the head is forced too tightly on the cap.

The paint that was applied to older bottles is very fragile and rubs off easily. Never scrub a bottle to clean it. In fact, with an older bottle, it may be more prudent to tolerate a little dirt than scrub off the paint. We speak from experience.

We have found that the best way to clean and protect the plastic containers is to gently dust the item with a soft cloth that has been liberally sprayed with Armor All. This will bring out the colors and actually protect the plastic against aging processes.

If possible, your soap bottles should be displayed in such a way that they are not exposed to ultra-violet sources (sunlight and fluorescent light), which will rapidly fade the colors and ultimately make the plastic more brittle.

NOTE: All pictures shown clockwise from top left unless otherwise noted.

Greg Moore has been active in collecting vintage toys for many years. His collection of bubble bath bottles is now over 650 strong and growing. Greg's interest in these containers began in 1993 with the purchase of a small collection of 16 Soakies from an antique mall. His Soaky collecting has become more of an obsession than a part-time hobby. He enjoys collecting these bottles because there is always something new coming out or old to discover to add to the collection. Greg works as manager of a garden center and is also the author of two other price guides on collectible toys. Greg resides in Castle Rock, Washington, with his wife Pam and daughters, Daphne and Tiffany.

Joe Pizzo first became interested in collecting Soakies when he had to find a way to encourage his three-year-old son to take a bath in the late 1960s. Together they accumulated an army of the plastic characters, which somehow have vanished. Many years later, Joe got a chance to rebuild his collection when he helped the Youth Rescue Mission of Beaumont clean out an old mansion. Scattered throughout the back of the house were 40 of the most collectible Soakies and Bubble Clubs, left by their original owner from the 1960s. Expanding on this base, Joe now has a collection of character-shaped bubble bath containers numbering well over 700. In his professional life, Joe is Regents' professor of physics at Lamar University. He resides in Beaumont, Texas, with his wife Bobbie Applegate.

Both authors welcome comments on this book as well as information about any bottles we may have failed to include. We would particularly like to hear from anyone associated with Purex or Colgate-Palmolive in the 1960s or 1970s, who might be able to fill in missing information about the production and distribution of the Soakies and Bubble Clubs. The authors can be contacted at:

Greg Moore
P.O. Box 1621
Castle Rock, WA 98611

Joe Pizzo
1675 Orange St.
Beaumont, TX 77701

e-mail: bapple@sat.net

CHAPTER 1

Mickey Mouse Bandleader
Colgate-Palmolive 1960s
R – 3 $25.00 – 30.00

Mouseketeer (variation)
Colgate-Palmolive 1960s
R – 3 $25.00 – 30.00

Mouseketeer (variation)
Colgate-Palmolive 1960s
R – 3 $25.00 – 30.00

Mickey Mouse
Colgate-Palmolive 1960s
R – 2 $8.00 – 12.00

NOTE: All pictures shown clockwise from top left unless otherwise noted.

Mickey Mouse
Centura (Canada) 1994
R – 2 $20.00 – 25.00

Minnie Mouse
Rosedew (England) 1989
R – 3 $25.00 – 30.00

Minnie Mouse
Centura (Canada) 1995
R – 2 $20.00 – 25.00

Minnie Mouse
Centura (Canada) 1994
R – 2 $20.00 – 25.00

Mickey Mouse
Centura (Canada) 1994
R – 2 $20.00 – 25.00

Mickey Mouse (Fantasia)
Centura (Canada) 1994
R – 2 $20.00 – 25.00

Mickey Mouse
Centura (Canada) 1994
R – 2 $20.00 – 25.00

Mickey Mouse
Rosedew (England) 1989
R – 3 $25.00 – 30.00

Minnie Mouse
Centura (Canada) 1994
R – 2 $20.00 – 25.00

Prince Mickey & Princess Minnie
Johnson & Johnson 1997
R – 1 $4.00 – 8.00 each

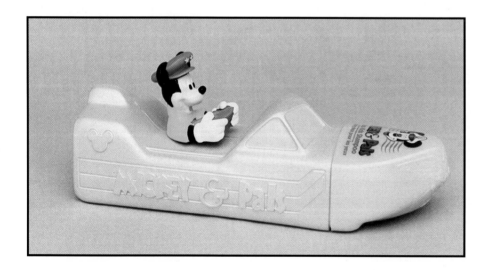

Mickey and Minnie Dancing
Grosvenor (England) 1997
R – 3 $20.00 – 25.00

Mickey Mouse Playing
Bongo Drum
Centura (Canada) 1996
R – 2 $15.00 – 20.00

Minnie Mouse Playing
Maracas
Centura (Canada) 1996
R – 2 $15.00 – 20.00

Mickey Mouse in Boat
Centura (Canada) 1995
R – 2 $10.00 – 15.00

Minnie Mouse in Boat
Centura (Canada) 1995
R – 2 $10.00 – 15.00

Donald Duck in Boat
Centura (Canada) 1995
R – 2 $10.00 – 15.00

Mickey Mouse Engineer
Johnson & Johnson 1996
R – 1 $5.00 – 10.00
Bottle fits under the train.

Goofy
Colgate-Palmolive 1960s
R – 2 $10.00 – 15.00

Goofy in Shower Stall
Centura (Canada) 1995
R – 2 $20.00 – 25.00

Donald Duck
Colgate-Palmolive 1960s
R – 3 $20.00 – 25.00

Pluto
Jamison 1950s
R – 3 $20.00 – 25.00

Pluto
Colgate-Palmolive 1960s
R – 2 $10.00 – 15.00

Donald Duck
Grosvenor (England) 1997
R – 3 $20.00 – 25.00

Donald Duck
Colgate-Palmolive 1960s
R – 2 $10.00 – 15.00

Donald Duck (variation)
Centura (Canada) 1995
R – 2 $20.00 – 25.00

Donald Duck (variation)
Centura (Canada) 1995
R – 2 $20.00 – 25.00

Snow White (movable arms)
Colgate-Palmolive 1960s
R – 3 $20.00 – 25.00

Snow White
Kid Care 1993
R – 1 $5.00 – 10.00

Snow White
Colgate-Palmolive 1960s
R – 3 $20.00 – 25.00

Snow White
Rosedew 1990s
R – 3 $25.00 – 30.00

Snow White
Centura (Canada) 1994
R – 2 $20.00 – 25.00

Snow White with animals
Grosvenor (England) 1995
R – 3 $25.00 – 30.00

**Dancing Dwarfs
(Dopey and Sneezy)
Grosvenor (England) 1995
R – 3 $25.00 – 30.00**

**Dopey (variation)
Colgate-Palmolive 1960s
R – 3 $15.00 – 20.00**

**Dopey (variation: slot in back)
Colgate-Palmolive 1960s
R – 3 $15.00 – 20.00**

**Cinderella (movable arms)
Colgate-Palmolive 1960s
R – 3 $20.00 – 25.00**

**Cinderella
Cosrich 1996
R – 1 $5.00 – 10.00**

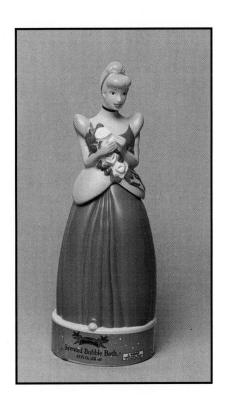

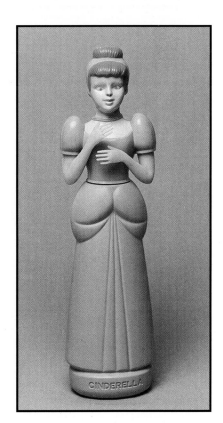

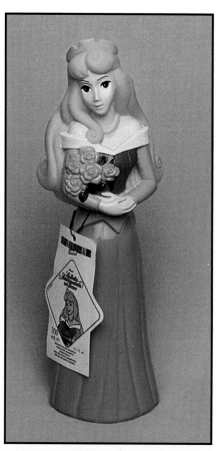

Cinderella
Damascar (Italy) 1996
R – 3 $25.00 – 30.00

Sleeping Beauty
Damascar (Italy) 1996
R – 3 $30.00 – 35.00

Pinocchio (variation)
Colgate-Palmolive 1960s
R – 2 $10.00 – 15.00

Pinocchio (variation)
Colgate-Palmolive 1960s
R – 2 $10.00 – 15.00

Pinocchio (variation)
Colgate-Palmolive 1960s
R – 2 $10.00 – 15.00

Jiminy Cricket (variation)
Colgate-Palmolive 1960s
R – 3 $15.00 – 20.00

Jiminy Cricket (variation)
Colgate-Palmolive 1960s
R – 2 $5.00 – 10.00

Baloo — Jungle Book
Boots (England) 1965
R – 5 $60.00 – 70.00

Baloo — Jungle Book
Colgate-Palmolive 1966
R – 2 $10.00 – 15.00
Soaky slip-over

King Louie — Jungle Book
Colgate-Palmolive 1960s
R – 3 $10.00 – 15.00
Soaky slip-over

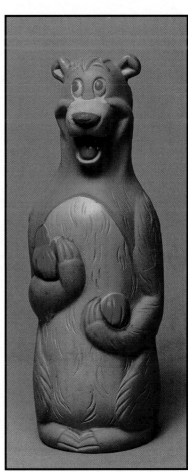

Mowgli & Kaa — Jungle Book
Prelude (England) 1995
R – 3 $25.00 – 30.00

Baloo — Jungle Book
Prelude (England) 1995
R – 3 $26.00 – 30.00

101 Dalmatians
Grosvenor (England) 1995
R – 3 $25.00 – 30.00

101 Dalmatians
Centura (Canada) 1996
R – 2 $20.00 – 25.00

101 Dalmatians — Pups
Grosvenor (England) 1997
R – 3 $20.00 – 25.00 ea.

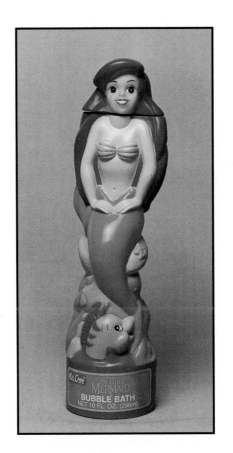

101 Dalmatians —
Dog House and Pups
Kid Care 1996
R – 1 $5.00 – 10.00

Little Mermaid
Kid Care 1991
R – 1 $4.00 – 8.00

Little Mermaid
Kid Care 1991
R – 1 $5.00 – 10.00

Little Mermaid
Johnson & Johnson 1997
R – 1 $3.00 – 6.00

Little Mermaid
Johnson & Johnson 1997
R – 1 $3.00 – 6.00

Little Mermaid in a Clamshell
Grosvenor (England) 1991
R – 3 $25.00 – 30.00

Little Mermaid
Damascar (Italy) 1996
R – 3 $25.00 – 30.00

Jasmine — Aladdin
Cosrich 1994
R – 1 $5.00 – 10.00

Genie — Aladdin
Cosrich 1995
R – 1 $5.00 – 10.00

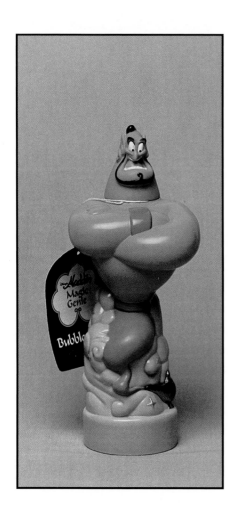

Nala — Lion King
Centura (Canada) 1994
R – 2 $20.00 – 25.00

Lion King
Kid Care 1995
R – 1 $5.00 – 10.00

Pumbaa — Lion King
Prelude (England) 1995
R – 3 $25.00 – 30.00

Simba on Rock
Prelude (England) 1995
R – 3 $25.00 – 30.00

Lion King & Cub on Pride Rock
Grosvenor (England) 1995
R – 3 $25.00 – 30.00

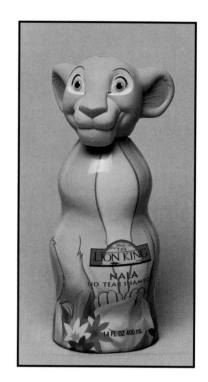

Pumbaa and Timon
Grosvenor (England) 1995
R – 3 $25.00 – 30.00

Simba — Lion King
Kid Care 1996
R – 1 $4.00 – 8.00

Nala — Lion King
Kid Care 1996
R – 1 $4.00 – 8.00

Belle — Beauty and the Beast
Centura (Canada) 1994
R – 2 $20.00 – 25.00

Belle — Beauty and the Beast
Prelude (England) 1994
R – 3 $25.00 – 30.00

Belle — Beauty and the Beast
Cosrich 1995
R – 1 $4.00 – 8.00

Beast — Beauty and the Beast
Cosrich 1995
R – 1 $4.00 – 8.00

Pocahontas
Kid Care 1995
R – 1 $4.00 – 8.00

Pocahontas (variations)
Grosvenor (England) 1996
R – 3 $30.00 – 35.00 ea.

John Smith
Centura (Canada) 1995
R – 2 $20.00 – 25.00

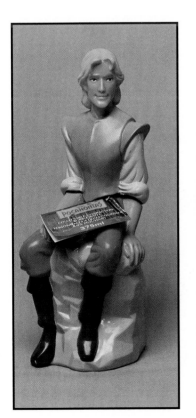

Pocahontas
Centura (Canada) 1995
R – 2 $20.00 – 25.00

Hunchback of Notre Dame
Grosvenor (England) 1996
R – 3 $30.00 – 35.00

Hunchback of Notre Dame
Kid Care 1996
R – 1 $5.00 – 10.00

Hunchback of Notre Dame
Funcare (Canada) 1996
R – 2 $20.00 – 25.00

Esmeralda
Kid Care 1996
R – 1 $5.00 – 10.00

Winnie the Pooh
Johnson & Johnson 1997
R – 1 $3.00 – 6.00
figure molded around bottle

Tigger, Pooh, and Eeyore
Grosvenor (England) 1997
R – 3 $25.00 – 30.00 ea.

Tigger on a Cart
Johnson & Johnson 1996
R – 1 $4.00 – 8.00
cart slips over bottle

Winnie the Pooh
Centura (Canada) 1995
R – 2 $20.00 – 25.00

Bambi
Colgate-Palmolive 1960s
R – 3 $20.00 – 25.00

Thumper
Colgate-Palmolive 1960s
R – 3 $20.00 – 25.00

Mighty Ducks
Cosrich 1996
R – 1 $4.00 – 8.00

Buzz Lightyear — Toy Story
Funcare (Canada) 1997
R – 1 $5.00 – 10.00

Baby Hercules and Pegasus
Funcare (Canada) 1997
R – 2 $15.00 – 20.00

Hercules
Kid Care 1997
R – 1 $4.00 – 8.00

CHAPTER 2

·····●● Hanna Barbera Characters ●●·····

Huckleberry Hound (10" variation)
Purex 1960s
R – 3 $25.00 – 30.00

Huckleberry Hound (10" variation)
Purex 1960s
R – 3 $25.00 – 30.00

Huckleberry Hound (15" variation)
Milvern 1960
R – 4 $45.00 – 50.00

Huckleberry Hound (10" variation)
John H. Gould LTD (England) 1960s
R – 5 $75.00 – 85.00

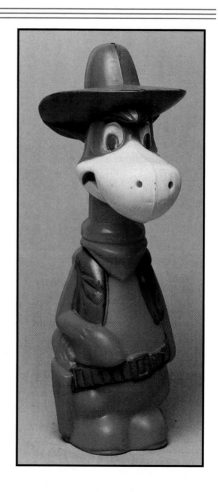

Quick Draw McGraw (variation)
Purex 1960s
R – 3 $25.00 – 30.00

Quick Draw McGraw
(El Cabong variation)
Purex 1960s
R – 5 $75.00 – 85.00

Quick Draw McGraw (variation)
Purex 1960s
R – 3 $25.00 – 30.00

Quick Draw McGraw (variation)
Purex 1960s
R – 3 $25.00 – 30.00

Quick Draw McGraw (variation)
Purex 1960s
R – 3 $25.00 – 30.00

Baba Looey (variation)
Purex 1960s
R – 3 $20.00 – 25.00

Baba Looey (variation)
Purex 1960s
R – 3 $15.00 – 20.00

Baba Looey (variation)
Roclar 1977
R – 2 $10.00 – 15.00
A large number of these exist mint
with tag from a warehouse find.

Yogi Bear (variation)
Purex 1960s
R – 3 $20.00 – 25.00

Yogi Bear (variation)
Purex 1960s
R – 3 $20.00 – 25.00

Yogi Bear (variation)
Purex 1960s
R – 3 $20.00 – 25.00

Yogi Bear
Damascar (Italy) 1995
R – 3 $30.00 – 35.00

Boo-Boo Bear
Damascar (Italy) 1995
R – 3 $30.00 – 35.00

Cindy Bear
Damascar (Italy) 1995
R – 3 $30.00 – 35.00

Fred Flintstone
Roclar 1970s
R – 3 $20.00 – 25.00

Barney Rubble (brown variation)
Roclar 1977
R – 2 $15.00 – 20.00 w/box
A large number of these exist mint
in box from a warehouse find.

Dino and Pebbles
Cosrich 1994
R – 2 $10.00 – 15.00

Fred Flintstone
Cosrich 1994
R – 2 $10.00 – 15.00

Barney Rubble (blue variation)
Milvern 1960s
R – 3 $20.00 – 25.00

Barney Rubble
Rosedew (England) 1993
R – 3 $25.00 – 30.00

Bamm-Bamm (variation)
Purex 1960s
R – 2 $15.00 – 20.00

Bamm-Bamm (variation)
Purex 1960s
R – 3 $20.00 – 25.00

Pebbles (variation)
Purex 1960s
R – 2 $10.00 – 15.00

Pebbles (variation)
Purex 1960s
R – 3 $20.00 – 25.00

Pebbles (variation)
Purex 1960s
R – 3 $20.00 – 25.00

Dino
Rosedew (England) 1993
R – 3 $25.00 – 30.00

Dino
Purex 1960s
R – 5 $75.00 – 85.00

Fred Flintstone
Rosedew (England) 1990s
R – 3 $30.00 – 35.00

Dino
Prelude (England) 1990s
R – 3 $30.00 – 35.00

Fred Flintstone
Rosedew (England) 1990s
R – 3 $30.00 – 35.00

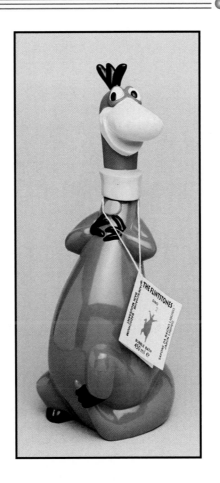

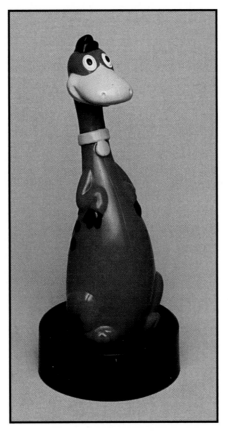

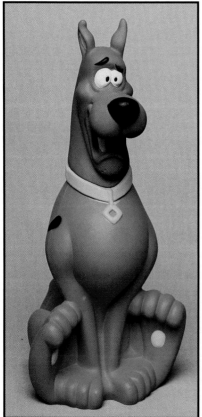

Secret Squirrel
Purex 1966
R – 4 $75.00 – 80.00

Morocco Mole
Purex 1966
R – 4 $80.00 – 90.00

Winsome Witch
Purex 1965
R – 4 $45.00 – 50.00

Squiddly Diddly
Purex 1965
R – 4 $60.00 – 70.00

Scooby Doo
Damascar (Italy) 1995
R – 3 $35.00 – 40.00

Scooby Doo
Colgate-Palmolive 1977
R – 3 $40.00 – 45.00

Scrappy Doo and Creature
Damascar (Italy) 1995
R – 3 $30.00 – 35.00

Magilla Gorilla (variation)
Purex 1960s
R – 4 $70.00 – 80.00

Magilla Gorilla (variation)
Purex 1960s
R – 4 $70.00 – 80.00

Magilla Gorilla (variation)
Purex 1960s
R – 4 $70.00 – 80.00

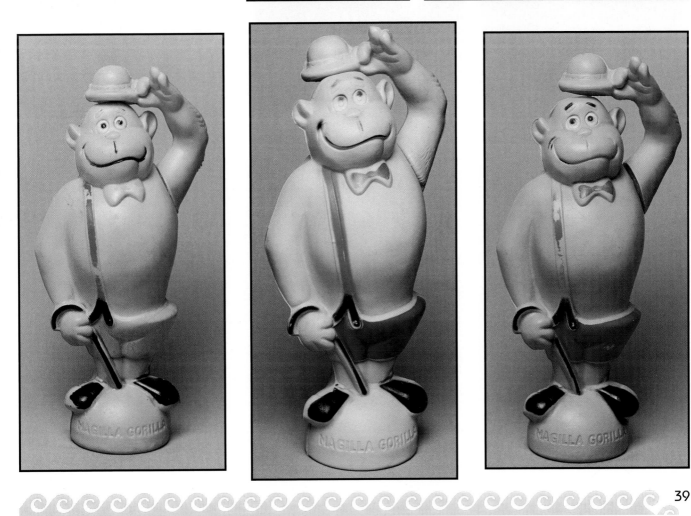

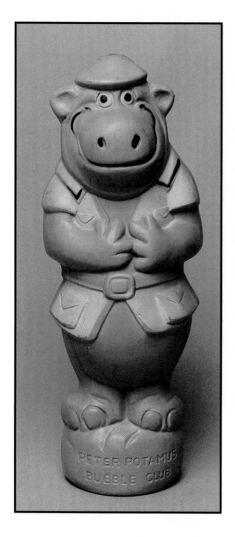

Peter Potamus (variation)
Purex 1960s
R – 4 $35.00 – 40.00

Peter Potamus (variation)
Roclar 1976
R – 2 $10.00 – 15.00
A large number of these exist mint
with tag from a warehouse find.

Yakky Doodle
Roclar 1970
R – 2 $10.00 – 15.00
A large number of these exist mint
with tag from a warehouse find.

Spouty Whale
Clark 1969
R – 2 $10.00 – 15.00
A large number of these exist mint
with tag from a warehouse find.

Touche Turtle
Purex 1964
R – 3 $30.00 – 35.00

Touche Turtle
(yellow feather variation)
Purex 1964
R – 3 $35.00 – 40.00

Punkin Puss (variation)
Purex 1966
R – 4 $45.00 – 50.00

Touche Turtle
(red feather variation)
Purex 1964
R – 4 $45.00 – 50.00

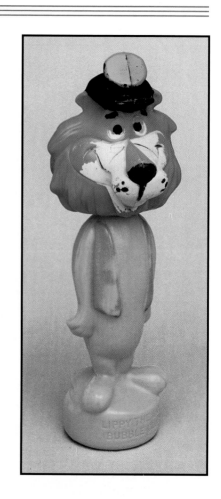

Snaggle Puss
Purex 1960s
R – 4 $40.00 – 50.00

Droop-a-Long Coyote
Purex 1960s
R – 4 $50.00 – 60.00

Lippy the Lion
Purex 1962
R – 4 $50.00 – 60.00

Mush Mouse
Purex 1960s
R – 4 $45.00 – 50.00

Punkin Puss (variation)
Purex 1966
R – 4 $45.00 – 50.00

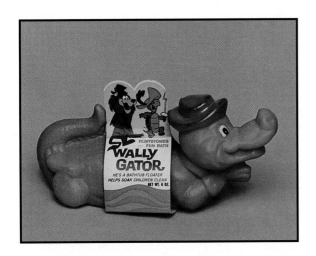

Wally Gator		
Clark 1969	R – 4	$60.00 – 70.00
Wally Gator		
Purex 1963	R – 4	$60.00 – 70.00
Ricochet Rabbit (movable arm variation)		
Purex 1964	R – 3	$35.00 – 40.00
Ricochet Rabbit (movable arm variation)		
Purex 1964	R – 3	$35.00 – 40.00
Ricochet Rabbit (non-movable arm variation)		
Purex 1960s	R – 4	$40.00 – 45.00

Breezly
Purex 1960s
R – 5 $125.00 – 150.00

Blabber Mouse
Purex 1960s
R – 5 $100.00 – 125.00

Sneezly
Purex 1960s
R – 5 $150.00 – 175.00

Top Cat (variation)
Colgate-Palmolive 1963
R – 3 $20.00 – 25.00

Top Cat (variation)
Colgate-Palmolive 1963
R – 3 $30.00 – 35.00

Atom Ant
Purex 1965
R – 4 $60.00 – 70.00

Auggie Doggie
Purex 1967
R – 4 $50.00 – 55.00

Dum Dum
Purex 1964
R – 5 $90.00 – 100.00

Jinx with Pixie and Dixie
Purex 1960s
R – 3 $25.00 – 30.00

CHAPTER 3

••• • ● Warner Bros. Characters ● • •••

Bugs Bunny
Colgate-Palmolive 1960s   R – 3 $20.00 – 25.00

Bugs Bunny (50th Anniversary)
DuCair Bioescence 1989   R – 2 $5.00 – 10.00

Bugs Bunny
Kid Care 1992   R – 2 $5.00 – 10.00

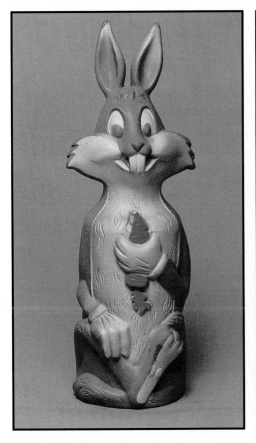

Bugs Bunny
Colgate-Palmolive 1960s
R – 3 $10.00 – 15.00
Soaky slip-over

Bugs Bunny
Colgate-Palmolive 1960s
R – 3 $15.00 – 20.00

Bugs Bunny
Minnetonka 1996
R – 1 $4.00 – 8.00

Bugs Bunny
DuCair Bioescence 1980s
R – 2 $8.00 – 12.00

Bugs Bunny
Minnetonka 1996
R – 1 $5.00 – 10.00

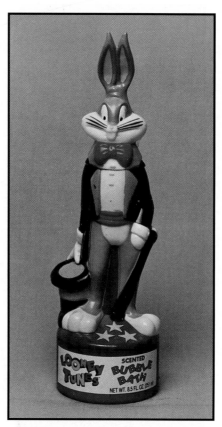

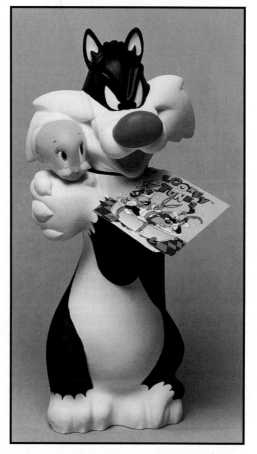

Bugs Bunny
Centura (Canada) 1994
R – 2 $20.00 – 25.00

Bugs Bunny
Cosrich 1980s
R – 2 $10.00 – 15.00

Sylvester
Colgate-Palmolive 1960s
R – 3 $25.00 – 30.00

Sylvester and Tweety
Minnetonka 1996
R – 1 $5.00 – 10.00

Sylvester and Tweety
DuCair Bioescence 1988
R – 3 $10.00 – 15.00

Sylvester and Tweety
Minnetonka 1996
R – 1 $4.00 – 8.00

Tweety
Colgate-Palmolive 1960s
R – 3 $15.00 – 20.00
Soaky slip-over

Tweety
Colgate-Palmolive 1960s
R – 3 $25.00 – 30.00

Tweety
Minnetonka 1996
R – 1 $5.00 – 10.00

Daffy Duck
Prelude (England) 1995
R – 3 $30.00 – 35.00

Daffy Duck
Minnetonka 1996
R – 1 $4.00 – 8.00

Tazmanian Devil
Prelude (England) 1997
R – 3 $25.00 – 30.00

Tazmanian Devil
Kid Care 1992
R – 2 $10.00 – 15.00

Tazmanian Devil
Minnetonka 1996
R – 1 $5.00 – 10.00

Tazmanian Devil
Centura (Canada) 1994
R – 2 $20.00 – 25.00

Tazmanian Devil
Cosrich 1994
R – 2 $10.00 – 15.00

Tazmanian Devil
Minnetonka 1996
R – 1 $4.00 – 8.00

Bugs Bunny
Warner Brothers Stores 1996
R – 2 $10.00 – 15.00

Sylvester and Tweety
Warner Brothers Stores 1996
R – 2 $10.00 – 15.00

Marvin the Martian
Warner Brothers Stores 1996
R – 2 $10.00 – 15.00

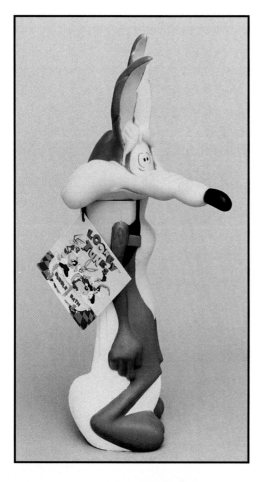

Wile E. Coyote
Minnetonka 1996
R – 1 $5.00 – 10.00

Elmer Fudd
Colgate-Palmolive 1960s
R – 3 $20.00 – 25.00

Speedy Gonzales
Colgate-Palmolive 1960s
R – 4 $30.00 – 35.00

Porky Pig (variation)
Colgate-Palmolive 1960s
R – 3 $20.00 – 25.00

Porky Pig (variation)
Colgate-Palmolive 1960s
R – 3 $25.00 – 30.00

CHAPTER 4

Public Broadcasting and Educational Television Characters

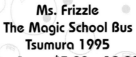

Ms. Frizzle
The Magic School Bus
Tsumura 1995
R – 1 $5.00 – 10.00

Mr. Do Bee — Romper Room
Manon Freres 1960s
R – 5 $60.00 – 70.00

Elmo
Kid Care 1997
R – 1 $5.00 – 10.00

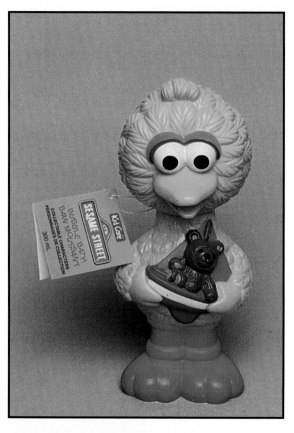

Big Bird
Kid Care 1997
R – 1 $5.00 – 10.00

Big Bird
(comes in 8½" and 9½" heights)
Softsoap 1992
R – 1 $4.00 – 8.00

Big Bird
Grosvenor (England) 1996
R – 3 $15.00 – 20.00

Big Bird in Pajamas
Minnetonka 1994
R – 1 $4.00 – 8.00

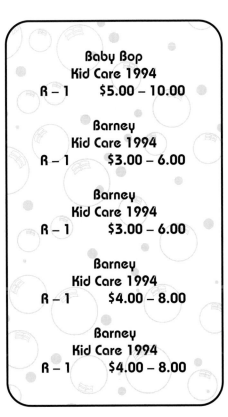

Baby Bop
Kid Care 1994
R – 1 $5.00 – 10.00

Barney
Kid Care 1994
R – 1 $3.00 – 6.00

Barney
Kid Care 1994
R – 1 $3.00 – 6.00

Barney
Kid Care 1994
R – 1 $4.00 – 8.00

Barney
Kid Care 1994
R – 1 $4.00 – 8.00

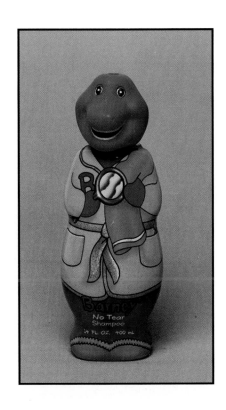

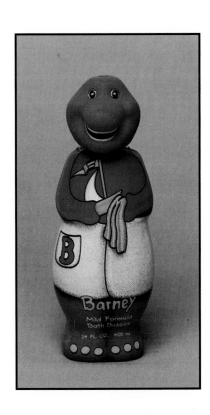

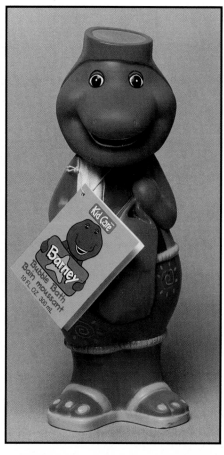

Barney
Kid Care 1994
R – 1 $4.00 – 8.00

Barney
Kid Care 1994
R – 1 $4.00 – 8.00

Miss Piggy
DuCair Bioescence 1988
R – 2 $10.00 – 15.00

Muppet Baby Miss Piggy
(England) 1980s
R – 3 $15.00 – 20.00

Muppet Baby Kermit the Frog
(England) 1980s
R – 3 $15.00 – 20.00

Miss Piggy
Muppet Treasure Island
Calgon 1996
R – 1 $5.00 – 10.00

Fozzie Bear
Muppet Treasure Island
Calgon 1996
R – 1 $5.00 – 10.00

Kermit the Frog
Muppet Treasure Island
Calgon 1996
R – 1 $5.00 – 10.00

Zoe
Minnetonka 1995
R – 1 $5.00 – 10.00

Elmo
Softsoap 1992
R – 1 $5.00 – 10.00

Prairie Dawn
Softsoap 1993
R – 1 $5.00 – 10.00

Ernie
Minnetonka 1994
R – 1 $5.00 – 10.00

Bert
Minnetonka 1995
R – 1 $5.00 – 10.00

Oscar the Grouch
Grosvenor (England) 1995
R – 3 $25.00 – 30.00

Oscar the Grouch
Minnetonka 1995
R – 1 $4.00 – 8.00

Cookie Monster
Grosvenor (England) 1995
R – 3 $25.00 – 30.00

Cookie Monster
Softsoap 1993
R – 1 $4.00 – 8.00

Thomas the Tank Engine
Grosvenor (England) 1992
R – 3 $25.00 – 30.00

James (Thomas' Friend)
Grosvenor (England) 1994
R – 3 $25.00 – 30.00

Florence
The Magic Roundabout
Grosvenor (England) 1993
R – 3 $25.00 – 30.00

Noddy
Grosvenor (England) 1992
R – 3 $25.00 – 30.00

Postman Pat
Rosedew (England) 1995
R – 3 $20.00 – 25.00

Postman Pat
Grosvenor (England) 1996
R – 3 $20.00 – 25.00

Postman Pat
Rosedew (England) 1995
R – 3 $20.00 – 25.00

Zebedee
The Magic Roundabout
Grosvenor (England) 1992
R – 3 $20.00 – 25.00

Mr. Plod
Grosvenor (England) 1994
R – 3 $20.00 – 25.00

Fireman Sam
Rosedew (England) 1993
R – 3 $25.00 – 30.00

Postman Pat's Cat on Mailbox
Rosedew (England) 1995
R – 3 $20.00 – 25.00

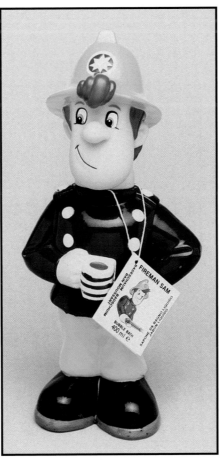

Pingu on an Igloo
Grosvenor (England) 1994
R – 3 $20.00 – 25.00

Spot
Grosvenor (England) 1993
R – 3 $15.00 – 20.00

Jim — Rosie and Jim Show
Rosedew (England) 1995
R – 3 $20.00 – 25.00

Tots TV
Euromark (England) 1996
R – 3 $20.00 – 25.00

CHAPTER 5

●●●● Cartoon and Comic Characters ●●●●

These characters are best known from their appearances in cartoons,
comic books, and/or newspaper comic pages.

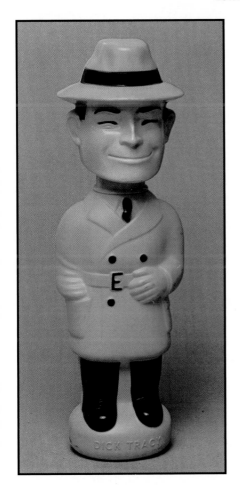

Dick Tracy
Colgate-Palmolive 1965   R – 3 $50.00 – 60.00

Little Orphan Annie
Lander Co. Inc. 1977   R – 3 $25.00 – 30.00

Broom Hilda
Lander Co. Inc. 1977   R – 4 $45.00 – 50.00

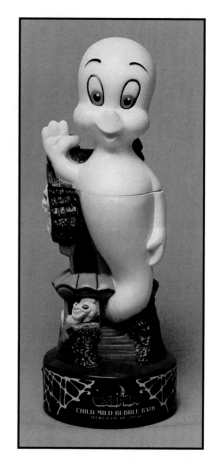

Casper
Colgate-Palmolive 1960s
R – 3 $25.00 – 30.00

Wendy
Colgate-Palmolive 1960s
R – 3 $25.00 – 30.00

Casper
Cosrich 1995
R – 1 $5.00 – 10.00

Casper
Euromark (England) 1995
R – 3 $25.00 – 30.00

Casper
Damascar (Italy) 1996
R – 3 $25.00 – 30.00

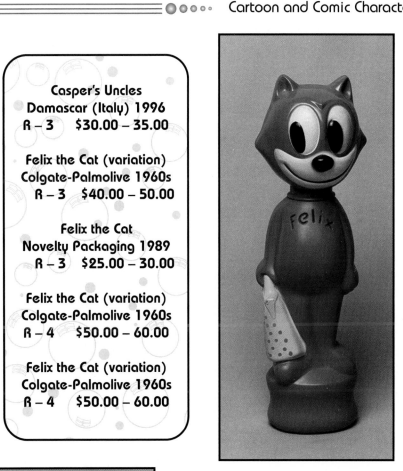

Casper's Uncles
Damascar (Italy) 1996
R – 3 $30.00 – 35.00

Felix the Cat (variation)
Colgate-Palmolive 1960s
R – 3 $40.00 – 50.00

Felix the Cat
Novelty Packaging 1989
R – 3 $25.00 – 30.00

Felix the Cat (variation)
Colgate-Palmolive 1960s
R – 4 $50.00 – 60.00

Felix the Cat (variation)
Colgate-Palmolive 1960s
R – 4 $50.00 – 60.00

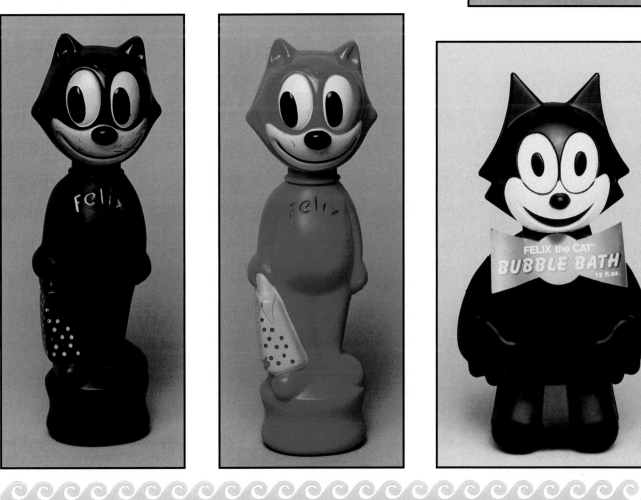

Deputy Dawg
Colgate-Palmolive 1960s
R – 2 　$10.00 – 15.00

Deputy Dawg
Colgate-Palmolive 1960s
R – 3 　$20.00 – 25.00

Tom and Jerry
Hollywood Trading Co. 1993
R – 2 　$5.00 – 10.00

Tom
Euromark (England) 1980
R – 3 　$30.00 – 35.00

Jerry and Tuffy
Damascar (Italy) 1990s
R – 3 　$30.00 – 35.00

Tom
Damascar (Italy) 1990s
R – 3 $30.00 – 35.00

Mighty Mouse
Colgate-Palmolive 1960s
R – 2 $25.00 – 30.00

Mighty Mouse
Colgate-Palmolive 1963
R – 2 $8.00 – 12.00

Mighty Mouse
Lander Co. Inc. 1978
R – 4 $45.00 – 50.00

Gumby
M & L Creative Packaging 1987
R – 2 $25.00 – 30.00

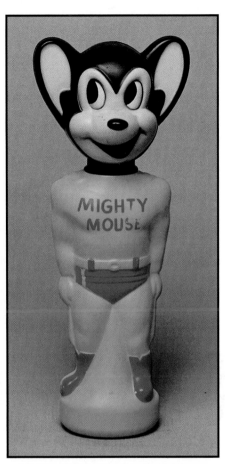

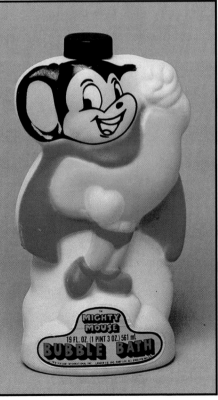

Blockhead
Novelty Packaging 1987
R – 4 $45.00 – 55.00

Pokey
Novelty Packaging 1987
R – 3 $35.00 – 40.00

Popeye
Colgate-Palmolive 1965
R – 3 $25.00 – 30.00

Popeye
Woolfoam 1960s
R – 3 $25.00 – 30.00

Popeye
Colgate-Palmolive 1977
R – 4 $35.00 – 40.00

Popeye
Rosedew (England) 1987
R – 4 $35.00 – 40.00

Popeye
Damascar (Italy) 1990s
R – 3 $40.00 – 45.00

Olive Oyl
Damascar (Italy) 1990s
R – 3 $40.00 – 45.00

Brutus
Damascar (Italy) 1990s
R – 3 $40.00 – 45.00

Brutus
Colgate-Palmolive 1965
R – 3 $30.00 – 35.00

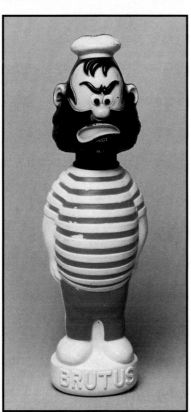

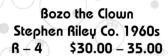

Bozo the Clown
Stephen Riley Co. 1960s
R – 4 $30.00 – 35.00

Bozo the Clown
Colgate-Palmolive 1960s
R – 3 $15.00 – 20.00

Mr. Magoo (variation)
Colgate-Palmolive 1960s
R – 3 $25.00 – 30.00

Mr. Magoo (variation)
Colgate-Palmolive 1960s
R – 3 $25.00 – 30.00

Alvin
Colgate-Palmolive 1960s
R – 2 $5.00 – 10.00

Alvin
DuCair Bioescence 1990
R – 3 $20.00 – 25.00

Alvin (variation)
Colgate-Palmolive 1960s
R – 3 $20.00 – 25.00

Alvin (variation)
Colgate-Palmolive 1960s
R – 3 $20.00 – 25.00

Alvin (variation)
Colgate-Palmolive 1960s
R – 3 $20.00 – 25.00

Alvin (variation)
Colgate-Palmolive 1960s
R – 3 $20.00 – 25.00

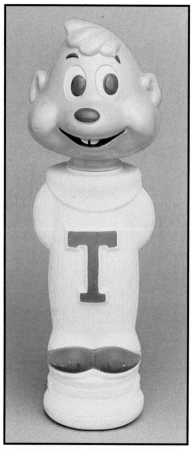

Simon (variation)
Colgate-Palmolive 1960s
R – 3 $20.00 – 25.00

Theodore (variation)
Colgate-Palmolive 1960s
R – 3 $20.00 – 25.00

Simon (variation)
Colgate-Palmolive 1960s
R – 3 $20.00 – 25.00

Simon (variation)
Colgate-Palmolive 1960s
R – 3 $20.00 – 25.00

Theodore (variation)
Colgate-Palmolive 1960s
R – 3 $20.00 – 25.00

Theodore (variation)
Colgate-Palmolive 1960s
R – 3 $20.00 – 25.00

Snoopy (Joe Cool)
Minnetonka 1996
R – 1 $5.00 – 10.00

Snoopy (Flying Ace)
Minnetonka 1996
R – 1 $5.00 – 10.00

Woodstock (Flying Ace)
Avon 1969
R – 3 $15.00 – 20.00

Snoopy (Beagle Scout)
Minnetonka 1996
R – 1 $5.00 – 10.00

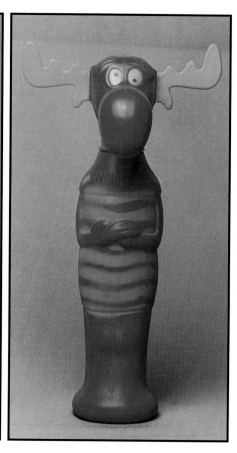

Rocky the Flying Squirrel
Colgate-Palmolive 1962
R – 3 $20.00 – 25.00

Bullwinkle (variation)
Colgate-Palmolive 1962
R – 3 $15.00 – 20.00

Bullwinkle (variation)
Colgate-Palmolive 1964
R – 3 $45.00 – 50.00

Bullwinkle (variation)
Colgate-Palmolive 1966
R – 3 $45.00 – 50.00

Bullwinkle (variation)
Colgate-Palmolive 1966
R – 3 $45.00 – 50.00

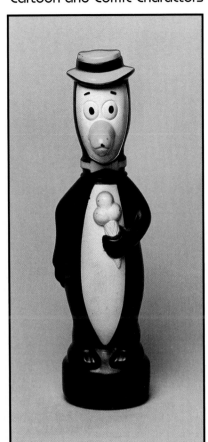

Bullwinkle
Fuller Brush Co. 1970s
R – 4 $50.00 – 60.00

Muskie
Colgate-Palmolive 1960s
R – 3 $25.00 – 30.00

Tennessee Tuxedo
Colgate-Palmolive 1965
R – 3 $20.00 – 25.00

Woody Woodpecker
Colgate-Palmolive 1960s
R – 2 $8.00 – 12.00

Woody Woodpecker
Colgate-Palmolive 1977
R – 3 $40.00 – 45.00

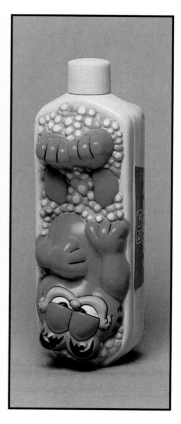

Tommy — Rugrats
Kid Care 1977
R – 1 $4.00 – 8.00

Pink Panther
Segura (Spain) 1995
R – 4 $35.00 – 40.00

Garfield
Kid Care 1990
R – 2 $10.00 – 15.00

Garfield
Grosvenor (England) 1981
R – 3 $30.00 – 35.00

Street Sharks
Kid Care 1996
R – 1 $5.00 – 10.00

Tiny Toon Adventures
Hollywood Trading Co. 1993
R – 2 $10.00 – 15.00

Sailor Moon
Cosrich 1996
R – 1 $5.00 – 10.00

Bart Simpson
Grosvenor (England) 1995
R – 3 $30.00 – 35.00

CHAPTER 6

Other Well Known Characters and Personalities

Dudley the Dragon
Cosrich 1994
R – 1 $5.00 – 10.00

Alf
PE (Germany) 1980s
R – 3 $30.00 – 35.00

Cecil — Beany and Cecil
Purex 1962
R – 3 $20.00 – 25.00

Lamb Chop
Kid Care 1993
R – 2 $5.00 – 10.00

Sonic the Hedgehog
Matey (England) 1991
R – 3 $30.00 – 35.00

Super Mario Brothers
Grosvenor (England) 1992
R – 3 $30.00 – 35.00

Super Mario Brothers
Novelty 1980s
R – 2 $8.00 – 12.00

Cowboys of Moo Mesa (D)
Kid Care 1992
R – 3 $10.00 – 15.00

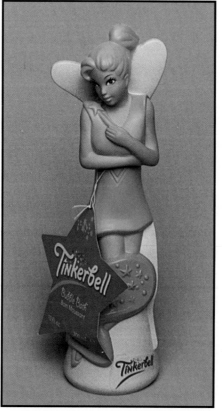

Cowboys of Moo Mesa (M)
Kid Care 1992
R – 3 $10.00 – 15.00

Cowboys of Moo Mesa (C)
Kid Care 1992
R – 3 $10.00 – 15.00

Tinkerbell (variation)
Tom Fields LTD (England)
R – 3 $30.00 – 35.00

Tinkerbell
Tinkerbell Inc. 1997
R – 1 $5.00 – 10.00

Tinkerbell (variation)
Tom Fields LTD (England)
R – 3 $30.00 – 35.00

Rockin' Raisin (variation)
Belvedere (Canada) 1980s
R – 2 $15.00 – 20.00

Rockin' Raisin (variation)
Belvedere (Canada) 1980s
R – 2 $15.00 – 20.00

Rockin' Raisin (variation)
Belvedere (Canada) 1980s
R – 2 $15.00 – 20.00

Mr. Wise
Wise Snack Foods
R – 5 $45.00 – 50.00

Woodsy Owl
Lander Co. Inc. 1970s
R – 4 $60.00 – 70.00

Smokey the Bear
Colgate-Palmolive 1960s
R – 2 $10.00 – 15.00

Smokey the Bear
Lander Co. Inc. 1970s
R – 3 $20.00 – 25.00

Big Bad Wolf
Tubby Time 1960s
R – 4 $35.00 – 40.00

Three Little Pig(s)
Tubby Time 1960s
R – 4 $30.00 – 35.00

Three Little Pig(s)
Tubby Time 1960s
R – 4 $30.00 – 35.00

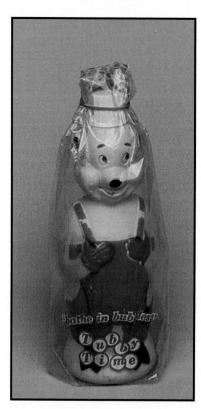

Three Little Pig(s)
Tubby Time 1960s
R – 4 $30.00 – 35.00

Anastasia
Kid Care 1997
R – 1 $4.00 – 8.00

Sindy
Rosedew (England) 1995
R – 3 $30.00 – 35.00

Pinocchio
(Holland) 1970s
R – 4 $40.00 – 45.00

Alice in Wonderland
Aidee (England) 1993
R – 3 $30.00 – 35.00

Sky Dancer on Dolphins Riding
a Wave
Euromark (England) 1996
R – 3 $20.00 – 25.00

Sky Dancer
Cosrich 1995
R – 1 $5.00 – 10.00

My Little Pony
Rockin' Beats Pony
Benjamin Ansehl 1990
R – 3 $15.00 – 20.00

My Little Pony
Merry Go Round Pony
Benjamin Ansehl 1990
R – 3 $15.00 – 20.00

Popples
DuCair Bioescence 1988
R – 2 $5.00 – 10.00

Popples
DuCair Bioescence 1988
R – 2 $5.00 – 10.00

Rainbow Brite
Hallmark 1995
R – 2 $8.00 – 10.00

Care Bear
A G C 1984
R – 2 $5.00 – 10.00

Care Bear
A G C 1984
R – 2 $5.00 – 10.00

Care Bear
A G C 1984
R – 2 $5.00 – 10.00

Holly Hobbie (variation)
Benjamin Ansehl 1980s
R – 2 $5.00 – 10.00

Holly Hobbie (variation)
Benjamin Ansehl 1980s
R – 3 $15.00 – 20.00

Sensations Barbie
DuCair Bioescence 1988
R – 2 $10.00 – 15.00

Barbie
Kid Care 1997
R – 1 $4.00 – 8.00

Rocker Barbie
DuCair Bioescence 1987
R – 3 $15.00 – 20.00

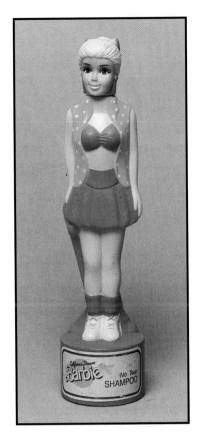

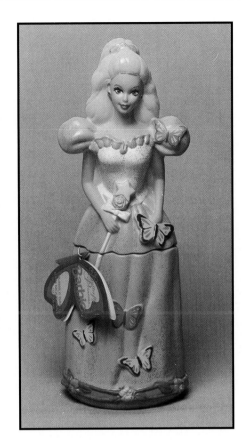

California Dream Barbie
DuCair Bioescence 1987
R – 2 $10.00 – 15.00

Camp Barbie
Kid Care 1994
R – 1 $5.00 – 10.00

Butterfly Princess Barbie
Kid Care 1995
R – 1 $5.00 – 10.00

Barbie
Grosvenor (England) 1994
R – 3 $25.00 – 30.00

Barbie
Grosvenor (England) 1995
R – 3 $25.00 – 30.00

Peter Rabbit in Watering Can
Grosvenor (England) 1996
R – 3 $20.00 – 25.00

The Tailor of Gloucester
Grosvenor (England) 1997
R – 3 $25.00 – 30.00

Benjamin Bunny
Grosvenor (England) 1990
R – 3 $20.00 – 25.00

Peter Rabbit
Grosvenor (England) 1990
R – 3 $10.00 – 15.00

Jemima Puddle Duck
Grosvenor (England) 1990
R – 3 $10.00 – 15.00

Ringo Starr
Colgate-Palmolive 1965
R – 3 $90.00 – 120.00

Paul McCartney
Colgate-Palmolive 1965
R – 3 $90.00 – 120.00

Mr. Blobby
Rosedew (England) 1992
R – 3 $20.00 – 25.00

Uncle Bulgaria — Wombles
Euromark (England) 1994
R – 3 $20.00 – 25.00

Magic Princess
Boots Co. (England) 1996
R – 3 $15.00 – 20.00

Wallace and Gromit
Euromark (England) 1996
R – 3 $25.00 – 30.00

Santa Claus
Colgate-Palmolive 1960s
R – 2 $15.00 – 20.00

Papa Smurf
I.M.P.S. (Belgium) 1994
R – 4 $30.00 – 35.00

Baker Smurf
I.M.P.S. (Belgium) 1991
R – 4 $30.00 – 35.00

EuroLion
Damascar (Italy) 1996
R – 3 $20.00 – 25.00

Desperate Dan
D.C. Thompson (England)
1990s
R – 3 $25.00 – 30.00

Edd the Duck
Euromark (England) 1990s
R – 3 $20.00 – 25.00

Troll
Euromark (England) 1990s
R – 3 $25.00 – 30.00

Bananas in Pajamas (B1 & B2)
Minnetonka 1997
R – 1 $5.00 – 10.00

Raggedy Ann
Lander Co. Inc. 1960s
R – 5 $55.00 – 65.00

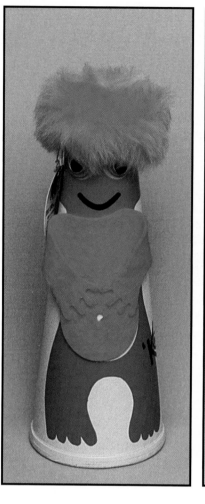

The Kook (Jerry Lewis Tie-in)
Maradel Products 1964
R – 5 $90.00 – 100.00

Gnasher — Dennis the Menace
Euromark (England) 1996
R- 3 $25.00 – 30.00

Gnasher — Dennis the Menace
Euromark (England) 1994
R- 3 $25.00 – 30.00

Budgie
Euromark (England) 1994
R- 3 $20.00 – 25.00

Flipper Riding a Wave
Euromark (England) 1996
R- 3 $20.00 – 25.00

Flipper Riding a Wave
Kid Care 1996
R – 1 $5.00 – 10.00

Paddington Bear
Cottsmore (England) 1992
R – 3 $25.00 – 30.00

Snowman
Grosvenor (England) 1990s
R – 3 $25.00 – 30.00

Jack Skellington behind Coffin
Nightmare before Christmas
Centura (Canada) 1994
R – 2 $15.00 – 20.00

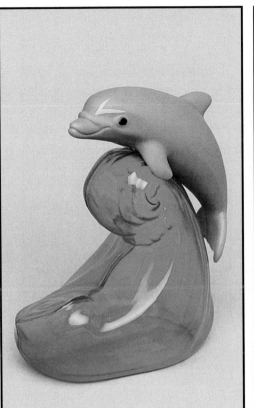

Polly Pocket's Castle
Centura (Canada) 1995
R – 2 $20.00 – 25.00

Mr. Happy
Rosedew (England) 1995
R – 3 $25.00 – 30.00

Mr. Funny
deLagar 1990s
R – 3 $25.00 – 30.00

Stan Laurel —
Plaster Cast Prototype
(no evidence of actual production)
Colgate-Palmolive (Soaky) 1960s

Oliver Hardy —
Plaster Cast Prototype
(no evidence of actual production)
Colgate-Palmolive (Soaky) 1960s

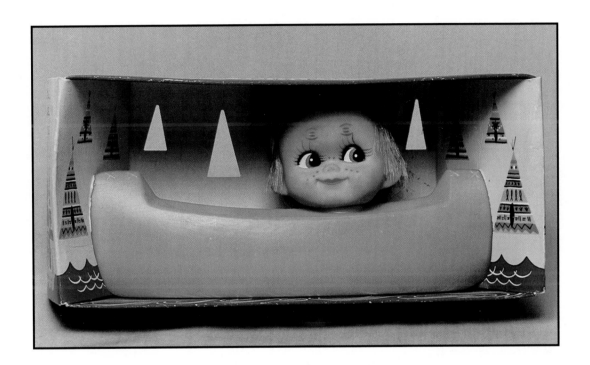

One Little Indian
Ansehl 1960s
R – 5 $20.00 – 25.00

Box for One Little Indian
Ansehl 1960s
R – 5 $30.00 – 35.00

ONE LITTLE INDIAN...
bubble bath
ONE LITTLE...TWO LITTLE...THREE LITTLE INDIANS!

13 FL. OZ.

IN RE-USABLE BATH TOY CANOE

For your Bubble Bath:
Pull up firmly on under side of doll head. Then unscrew plastic cap and pour one ounce of Bubble Bath under fast running water. Use as a toy too. When empty fill canoe with enough water so it floats properly.

ANSEHL CO. • ST. LOUIS, MO. U.S.A. 63147

Snork Boy
Plantschi (Germany) 1989
R – 3 $25.00 – 30.00

Snork Girl
Plantschi (Germany) 1989
R – 3 $25.00 – 30.00

Percy the Penguin
Cleftwood 1960s
R – 4 $25.00 – 30.00

Uncle Suds
Koscot 1972
R – 5 $40.00 – 45.00

Musical Bear with Drum
deLagar 1980s
R – 3 $10.00 – 15.00

Musical Bear with Baton
deLagar 1980s
R – 3 $10.00 – 15.00

Musical Bear with Accordion
deLagar 1980s
R – 3 $10.00 – 15.00

Checks Chipmunk
Benjamin Ansehl 1990s
R – 2 $8.00 – 12.00

Scoots Squirrel
Benjamin Ansehl 1990s
R – 2 $8.00 – 12.00

Skates Turtle
Benjamin Ansehl 1990s
R – 2 $8.00 – 12.00

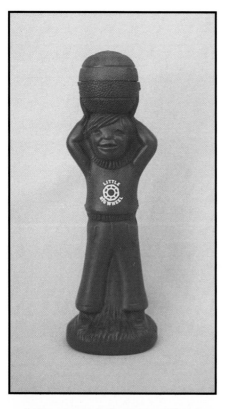

Little Big Wheel
Stanley Home Products
R – 4 $5.00 – 10.00

Angler
Boots Co. (England) 1995
R – 3 $25.00 – 30.00
This bottle contained a mixture of
bubble bath and liniment called
muscle soak.

Rugby Player
Boots Co. (England) 1995
R – 3 $25.00 – 30.00
There is a button on the back of
this bottle that activates a musical
chip which plays a team song.

Football (Soccer) Player
Boots Co. (England) 1995
R – 3 $25.00 – 30.00
There is a button on the back of
this bottle that activates a musical
chip which plays a team song.

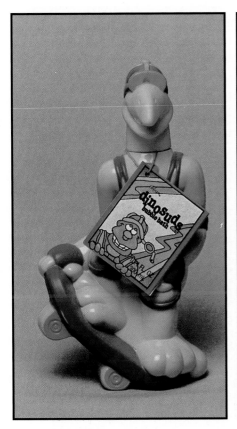

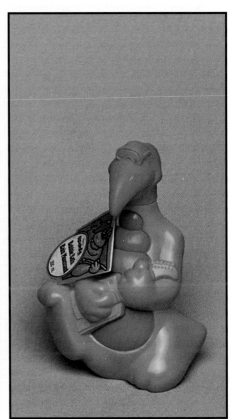

Dinosuds Dinosaur
deLagar (Canada) 1990
R – 1 $5.00 – 10.00

Dinosuds Dinosaur
deLagar (Canada) 1990
R – 1 $5.00 – 10.00

Dinosuds Dinosaur
deLagar (Canada) 1990
R – 1 $5.00 – 10.00

Dinosuds Dinosaur
deLagar (Canada) 1990
R – 1 $5.00 – 10.00

Dinosuds Dinosaur
deLagar (Canada) 1990
R – 1 $5.00 – 10.00

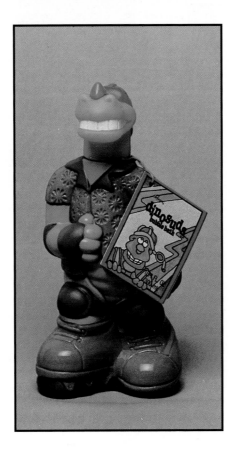
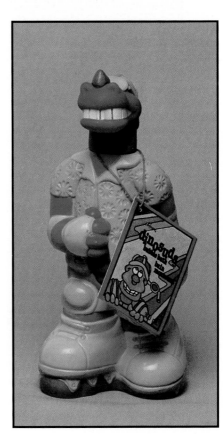

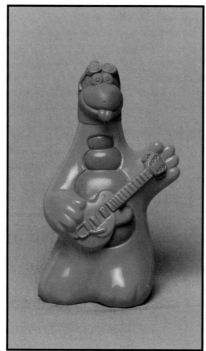

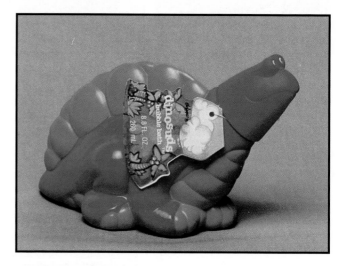

Dinosuds Dinosaur • deLagar (Canada) 1990	
R – 1	$5.00 – 10.00
Dinosuds Dinosaur • deLagar (Canada) 1990	
R – 1	$5.00 – 10.00
Dinosuds Dinosaur • deLagar (Canada) 1990	
R – 1	$5.00 – 10.00
Dinosuds Dinosaur • deLagar (Canada) 1990	
R – 1	$5.00 – 10.00
Dinosuds Dinosaur • deLagar (Canada) 1990	
R – 1	$5.00 – 10.00

Blue Owl
Lander Co. Inc. 1990
R – 1 $2.00 – 3.00

Green Owl
Lander Co. Inc. 1990
R – 1 $2.00 – 3.00

Pink Owl
Lander Co. Inc. 1990
R – 1 $2.00 – 3.00

Blue Dinosaur
Lander Co. Inc. 1990
R – 1 $2.00 – 3.00

Green Dinosaur
Lander Co. Inc. 1990
R – 1 $2.00 – 3.00

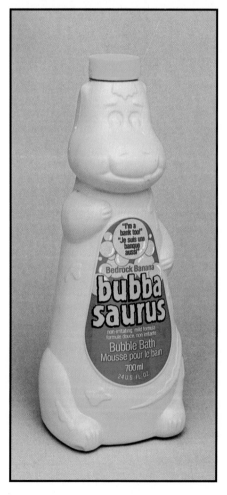

Green Turtle
Lander Co. Inc. 1990
R – 1 $2.00 – 3.00

Blue Bear
Lander Co. Inc. 1990
R – 1 $2.00 – 3.00

Pink Bear
Lander Co. Inc. 1990
R – 1 $2.00 – 3.00

Bubbasaurus
Belvedere (Canada) 1990s
R – 2 $5.00 – 10.00

Bubbasaurus
Belvedere (Canada) 1990s
R – 2 $5.00 – 10.00

Bubbasaurus
Belvedere (Canada) 1990s
R – 2 $5.00 – 10.00

Bubbasaurus
Belvedere (Canada) 1990s
R – 2 $5.00 – 10.00

Bubbly Bear
Belvedere (Canada) 1995
R – 2 $5.00 – 10.00

Bubbly Bear
Belvedere (Canada) 1995
R – 2 $5.00 – 10.00

Warrior Dude
Belvedere (Canada) 1990s
R – 3 $10.00 – 15.00

Warrior Dude
Belvedere (Canada) 1990s
R – 3 $10.00 – 15.00

Pink Kangaroo
Ansehl
R – 3 $10.00 – 15.00

Fantasti-Cat
Ansehl
R – 3 $10.00 – 15.00

Fantasti-Cat
Ansehl
R – 3 $10.00 – 15.00

White Pampered Poodle
Ansehl
R – 3 $10.00 – 15.00

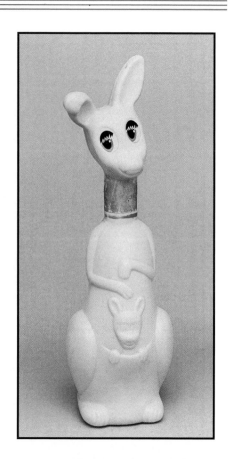

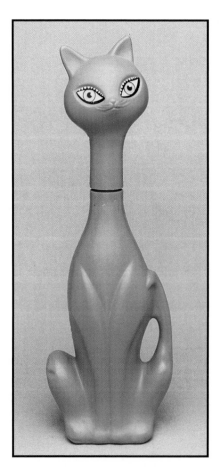

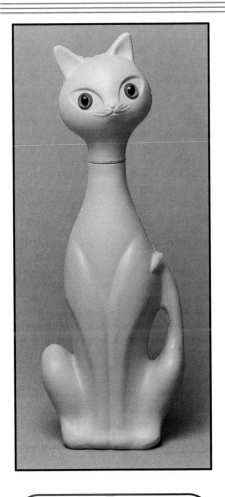

Fantasti-Cat
Ansehl
R – 3 $10.00 – 15.00

Black Pampered Poodle
Ansehl
R – 3 $10.00 – 15.00

Pink Cat
DPG Drugs
R – 3 $15.00 – 20.00

Tan Kangaroo
Ansehl
R – 3 $10.00 – 15.00

Pink Squirrel
R – 3 $10.00 – 15.00

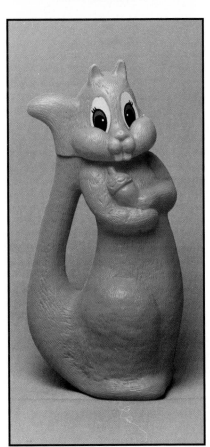

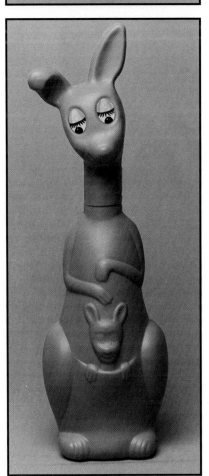

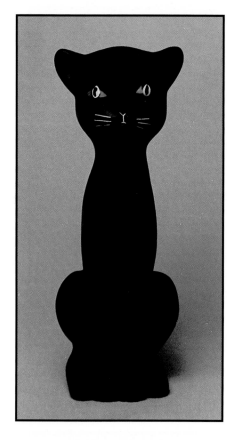

**Black Cat
Niagra**
R – 3 $5.00 – 10.00

Copper Dog
R – 3 $5.00 – 10.00

**Dr. Snuggles
O'Kelly**
R – 4 $25.00 – 30.00

Teddy in my Pocket
(Bear on a honey jar)
Euromark (England) 1996
R – 3 $20.00 – 25.00
A toy figure inside the bubble
bath is included as a prize.

**Pink Flamingo
Benjamin Ansehl 1990s**
R – 2 $5.00 – 10.00

Leo Lion
Belvedere (Canada) 1990s
R – 3 $5.00 – 10.00

Bear
Tubby Time 1960s
R – 4 $40.00 – 45.00

Dog
Tubby Time 1960s
R – 4 $40.00 – 45.00

Lamb
Tubby Time 1960s
R – 4 $40.00 – 45.00

Li'l Bear
A & AG (Canada) 1990s
R – 3 $5.00 – 10.00

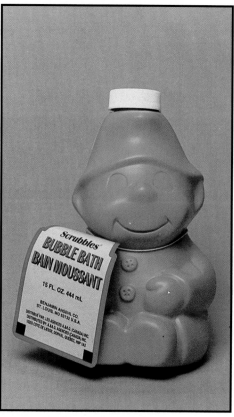

Li'l Bear
A & AG (Canada) 1990s
R – 3 $5.00 – 10.00

Scrubbles
Benjamin Ansehl 1995
R – 2 $5.00 – 10.00

Zeddy
Zeller's (Canada) 1990s
R – 2 $5.00 – 10.00
These containers were filled with
different colors of bubble bath.

Clown
Jergans 1960s
R – 3 $10.00 – 15.00

Bobo Bubbles
Lander Co. Inc. 1950s
R – 4 $25.00 – 30.00

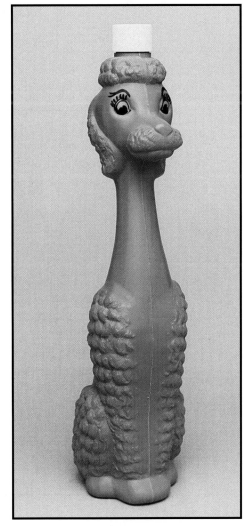

Pink Clown
R – 3 $5.00 – 10.00

Blue Clown
R – 3 $5.00 – 10.00

Forever Friends
Grosvenor (England) 1995
R – 3 $15.00 – 20.00

Blue Poodle
R – 3 $15.00 – 20.00

Penguin
R – 3 $15.00 – 20.00

Cuddle Bear
Superior Products 1995
R – 1 $1.00 – 3.00

Pig (Porky?)
Blair
R – 3 $8.00 – 12.00

Red Fish
Burnus (Germany)
R – 3 $5.00 – 10.00

Yellow Fish
Burnus (Germany)
R – 3 $5.00 – 10.00

Swan
Burnus (Germany)
R – 3 $5.00 – 10.00

Blue Dolphin • Burnus (Germany)
R – 3 $5.00 – 10.00

Frog • Euromark (England) 1996
R – 3 $10.00 – 15.00

Duck • Burnus (Germany)
R – 3 $5.00 – 10.00

Duck • Euromark (England) 1996
R – 3 $10.00 – 15.00

CHAPTER 8

•••• ● Heroes, Super Heroes, and Warriors ● ••••

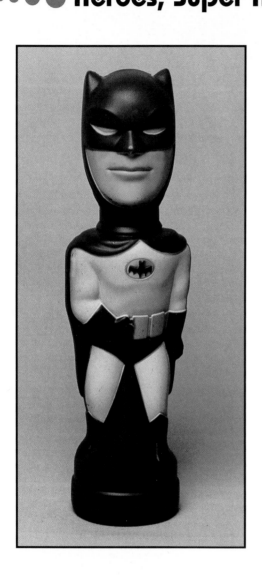 

Batman • Colgate-Palmolive 1966
R – 3 $50.00 – 60.00

Robin • Colgate-Palmolive 1966
R – 4 $60.00 – 70.00

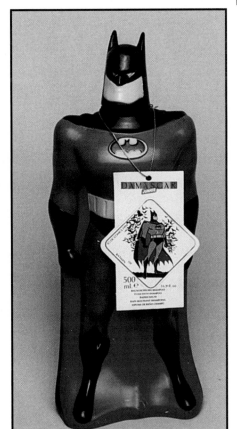

Batman
Kid Care 1995
R – 1 $5.00 – 10.00

Batman — Batman Forever
Prelude (England) 1995
R – 3 $25.00 – 30.00

Batman
Kid Care 1991
R – 1 $5.00 – 10.00

Robin
Kid Care 1995
R – 1 $5.00 – 10.00

Batman (animated)
Damascar (Italy) 1994
R – 3 $30.00 – 35.00

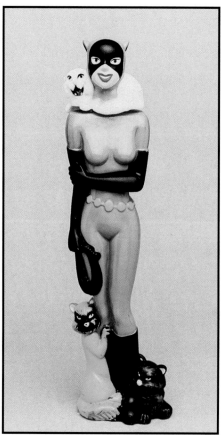

Batman
Damascar (Italy) 1995
R – 3 $35.00 – 40.00

Catwoman
Damascar (Italy) 1995
R – 3 $40.00 – 45.00

Robin
Damascar (Italy) 1994
R – 3 $35.00 – 40.00

Superman
Colgate-Palmolive 1965
R – 3 $40.00 – 50.00

Superman
Avon 1978
R – 2 $8.00 – 12.00
without cape
$15.00 – 20.00 with cape

Superman
Damascar (Italy) 1995
R – 3 $35.00 – 40.00

Superman
Euromark (England) 1994
R – 3 $30.00 – 35.00

Superman (animated)
Kid Care 1996
R – 1 $5.00 – 10.00

Michelangelo — Ninja Turtle
Kid Care 1991
R – 1 $4.00 – 8.00

Michelangelo — Ninja Turtle
Kid Care 1993
R – 1 $4.00 – 8.00

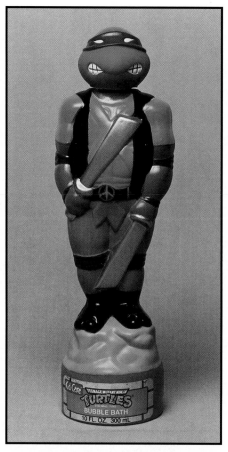

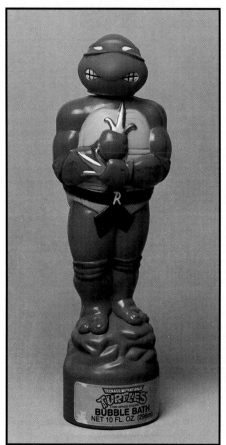

Leonardo — Ninja Turtle
Kid Care 1991
R – 1 $4.00 – 8.00

Leonardo — Ninja Turtle
Kid Care 1993
R – 1 $4.00 – 8.00

Donatello — Ninja Turtle
Kid Care 1989
R – 1 $5.00 – 10.00

Donatello — Ninja Turtle
Kid Care 1991
R – 1 $5.00 – 10.00

Raphael — Ninja Turtle
Kid Care 1989
R – 1 $4.00 – 8.00

Yellow Power Ranger
Centura (Canada) 1994
R – 2 $15.00 – 20.00

Pink Power Ranger
Centura (Canada) 1994
R – 2 $15.00 – 20.00

Blue Power Ranger
Centura (Canada) 1994
R – 2 $15.00 – 20.00

Black Power Ranger
Kid Care 1994
R – 1 $5.00 – 10.00

Red Power Ranger
Kid Care 1994
R – 1 $5.00 – 10.00

Pink Power Ranger
Kid Care 1994
R – 1 $5.00 – 10.00

White Power Ranger
Kid Care 1994
R – 1 $5.00 – 10.00

Blue Power Ranger
Kid Care 1994
R – 1 $5.00 – 10.00

GI Joe — Storm Shadow
DuCair Bioescence 1980s
R – 3 $10.00 – 15.00

GI Joe — Drill Instructor
DuCair Bioescence 1980s
R – 3 $10.00 – 15.00

GI Joe — Warrant Officer
DuCair Bioescence 1980s
R – 3 $10.00 – 15.00

GI Joe — Missile Specialist
DuCair Bioescence 1980s
R – 3 $10.00 – 15.00

GI Joe — Tan Camouflage
DuCair Bioescence 1980s
R – 3 $10.00 – 15.00

GI Joe Canteen
DuCair Bioescence 1987
R – 3 $10.00 – 15.00

GI Joe Telephone
Kid Care 1991
R – 3 $10.00 – 15.00

GI Joe Telephone
DuCair Bioescence 1989
R – 3 $10.00 – 15.00

James Bond
(Roger Moore)
BRB (England) 1970s
R – 5 $100.00 – 120.00

Action Man —
Space Commando
Rosedew (England) 1994
R – 3 $20.00 – 25.00

Action Man —
Battle Force
Rosedew (England) 1994
R – 3 $20.00 – 25.00

Action Man —
VR Warrior
Grosvenor (England) 1996
R – 3 $20.00 – 25.00

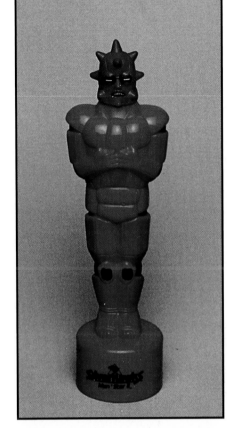

Samurai Syber Warrior
Cosrich 1994
R – 1 $5.00 – 10.00

Mon*Star II — Silverhawks
DuCair Bioescence 1986
R – 4 $20.00 – 25.00

Marshall Bravestarr
DuCair Bioescence 1986
R – 4 $20.00 – 25.00

Tex Hex — Bravestarr
DuCair Bioescence 1986
R – 4 $20.00 – 25.00

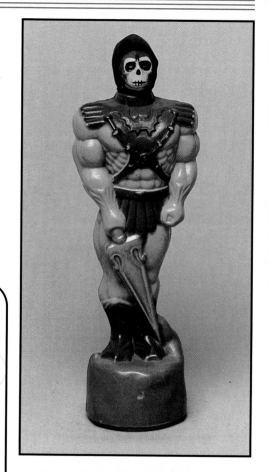

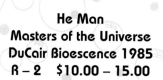

He Man
Masters of the Universe
DuCair Bioescence 1985
R – 2 $10.00 – 15.00

Skeletor
Masters of the Universe
DuCair Bioescence 1985
R – 2 $10.00 – 15.00

Skeleton Warriors
Cosrich 1994
R – 1 $5.00 – 10.00

Skeleton Warriors
Cosrich 1994
R – 1 $5.00 – 10.00

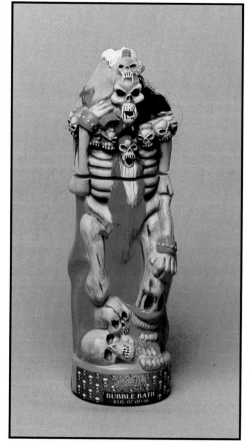

Ultimate Warrior
Grosvenor (England) 1991
R – 3 $20.00 – 25.00

Hulk Hogan
("Hulk Rules" on shirt)
Markham (Canada) 1986
R – 2 $15.00 – 20.00

Hulk Hogan
("Hulkamania" on shirt)
Fulford (Canada) 1986
R – 2 $15.00 – 20.00

CHAPTER 9

•• Science Fiction, Space, Fantasy, and Monsters ••

R2-D2 — Star Wars • Omni 1981
R – 2 $15.00 – 20.00

Yoda — Star Wars • Omni 1981
R – 2 $15.00 – 20.00

Star Wars Refueling Station
Omni 1982
R – 4 $10.00 – 15.00
"Keep one or more on
hand to make sure your
kids always have Luke Skywalker, R2-D2, Yoda, and
Darth Vader ready when
it's shampoo time."

Darth Vader
Star Wars
Omni 1981
R – 2 $15.00 – 20.00

Luke Skywalker
Star Wars
Omni 1981
R – 2 $15.00 – 20.00

Jabba the Hut
Star Wars
Omni 1981
R – 2 $15.00 – 20.00

Wicket the Ewok
Star Wars
Omni 1981
R – 2 $15.00 – 20.00

Chewbacca — Star Wars
Omni 1981
R – 2 $15.00 – 20.00

Princess Leia — Star Wars
Omni 1981
R – 2 $15.00 – 20.00

Darth Vader — Star Wars
Cliro (England) 1978
R – 5 $55.00 – 65.00

R2-D2 — Star Wars
Cliro (England) 1978
R – 4 $45.00 – 55.00

Darth Vader — Star Wars
Grosvenor (England) 1995
R – 3 $25.00 – 30.00

U.S.S. Enterprise — Star Trek
Euromark (England) 1994
R – 3 $25.00 – 30.00

First Contact — Star Trek
Cosrich 1996
R – 1 $4.00 – 8.00

Gold Astrosnik
DuCair Bioescence 1984
R – 2 $10.00 – 15.00

Purple Astrosnik
DuCair Bioescence 1984
R – 2 $10.00 – 15.00

Display Case of 12 Astrosniks

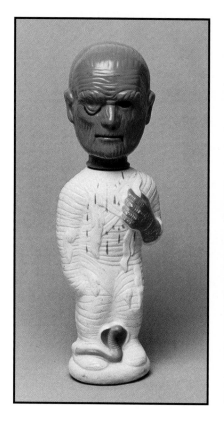

The Mummy
Colgate-Palmolive 1963
R – 3 $90.00 – 110.00

Creature from the Black Lagoon
Colgate-Palmolive 1963
R – 3 $100.00 – 120.00

Wolfman
(blue pants variation)
Colgate-Palmolive 1963
R – 3 $80.00 – 100.00

Wolfman
(red pants variation)
Colgate-Palmolive 1963
R – 3 $80.00 – 100.00

Frankenstein
Colgate-Palmolive 1963
R – 3 $80.00 – 90.00

Frankenstein
(Horror Bubbles)
Jackel (England) 1994
R – 3 $30.00 – 35.00

Dracula
(Horror Bubbles)
Jackel (England) 1994
R – 3 $30.00 – 35.00

Computer Robot
Ansehl 1980s
R – 4 $10.00 – 15.00

Computer Robot
Ansehl 1980s
R – 4 $10.00 – 15.00

Computer Robot
Ansehl 1980s
R – 4 $10.00 – 15.00

Computer Robot
Ansehl 1980s
R – 4 $10.00 – 15.00

Dalek — Dr. Who
(England) 1960s
R – 4 $25.00 – 30.00

RoboCop
Cosway 1990
R – 2 $10.00 – 15.00

RoboCop
Euromark (England) 1990
R – 2 $30.00 – 35.00

Mask
Prelude (England) 1996
R – 3 $25.00 – 30.00

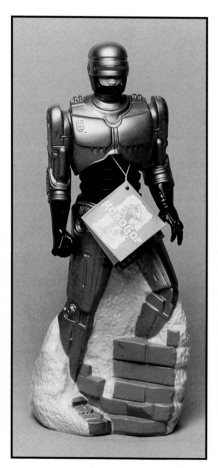

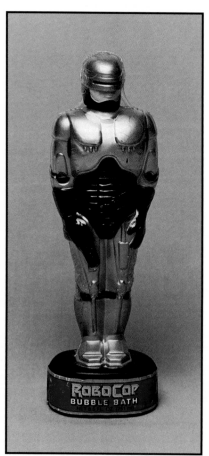

Dragonheart
Cosrich 1996
R – 1 $4.00 – 8.00

Captain Scarlet
Euromark (England) 1993
R – 3 $25.00 – 30.00

Victory 1 Spaceship
Benjamin Ansehl 1988
R – 3 $20.00 – 25.00

Space Shuttle
Kid Care 1980s
R – 4 $25.00 – 30.00

Arrow Star Rocket
R – 4 $20.00 – 25.00

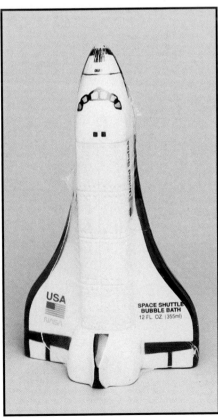

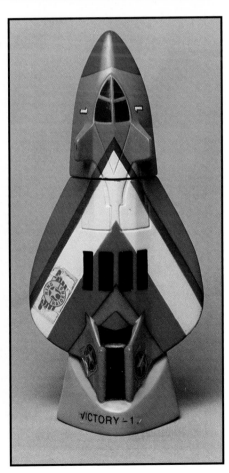

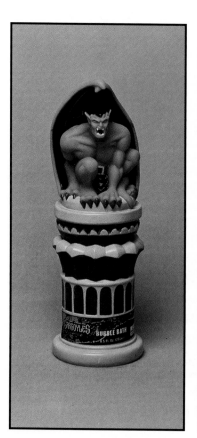

Biker Mice from Mars
Grosvenor (England) 1994
R – 3 $25.00 – 30.00

E.T.
Avon 1984
R – 3 $10.00 – 15.00

King Kong (?)
The Louangel Corporation
1970s
R – 3 $10.00 – 15.00

Jurassic Park
Cosrich 1992
R – 2 $5.00 – 10.00

Gargoyles
Cosrich 1995
R – 1 $4.00 – 8.00

CHAPTER 10

●●●● Elegant Women ●●●●

Fairy Godmother (variation) • deLagar (Canada) 1994
R – 3 $20.00 – 25.00

Fairy Godmother (variation) • deLagar (Canada) 1994
R – 3 $20.00 – 25.00

Mermaid (variation) • deLagar (Canada) 1994
R – 3 $20.00 – 25.00

Mermaid (variation)
deLagar (Canada) 1994
R – 3 $20.00 – 25.00

Surfer
deLagar (Canada) 1997
R – 2 $10.00 – 15.00

Native American
deLagar (Canada) 1997
R – 2 $10.00 – 15.00

Pioneer
deLagar (Canada) 1997
R – 2 $10.00 – 15.00

Betty Bubbles
Lander Co. Inc. 1960s
R – 3 $10.00 – 15.00

Betty Bubbles
Lander Co. Inc. 1950s
R – 3 $10.00 – 15.00

Betty Bubbles
Lander Co. Inc. 1960s
R – 3 $10.00 – 15.00

Betty Bubbles
Lander Co. Inc. 1950s
R – 3 $10.00 – 15.00

Betty Bubbles
Lander Co. Inc. 1950s
R – 3 $10.00 – 15.00

Betty Bubbles
Lander Co. Inc. 1960s
R – 3 $10.00 – 15.00

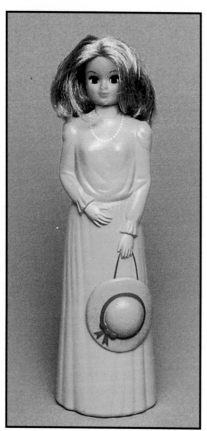

Betty Bubbles
Lander Co. Inc. 1950s
R – 3 $10.00 – 15.00

Betty Bubbles
Lander Co. Inc. 1950s
R – 3 $10.00 – 15.00

Betty Bubbles
Lander Co. Inc. 1960s
R – 3 $10.00 – 15.00

deLagar Woman
deLagar (Canada) 1991
R – 2 $10.00 – 15.00

deLagar Woman
deLagar (Canada) 1993
R – 2 $10.00 – 15.00

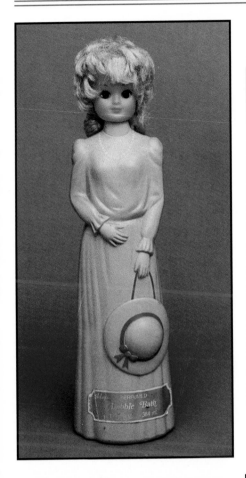

deLagar Woman
deLagar (Canada) 1993
R – 2 $10.00 – 15.00

deLagar Woman
deLagar (Canada) 1994
R – 2 $15.00 – 20.00

deLagar Woman
deLagar (Canada) 1989
R – 2 $15.00 – 20.00

deLagar Woman
deLagar (Canada) 1993
R – 2 $10.00 – 15.00

deLagar Woman
deLagar (Canada) 1989
R – 2 $10.00 – 15.00

deLagar Woman
deLagar (Canada) 1989
R – 2 $10.00 – 15.00

deLagar Woman
deLagar (Canada) 1993
R – 2 $15.00 – 20.00

deLagar Woman
deLagar (Canada) 1991
R – 2 $15.00 – 20.00

deLagar Woman
deLagar (Canada) 1993
R – 2 $15.00 – 20.00

deLagar Woman
deLagar (Canada) 1993
R – 2 $15.00 – 20.00

CHAPTER 11

●●●● Vehicles and Other Things ●●●●

Fire Truck (Pumper)
Colgate-Palmolive
(Soaky Speed Toy) 1960s
R – 3 $25.00 – 30.00

Fire Truck (Ladder)
Colgate-Palmolive
(Soaky Speed Toy) 1960s
R – 3 $25.00 – 30.00

Gravel Truck
Colgate-Palmolive
(Soaky Speed Toy) 1960s
R – 4 $25.00 – 30.00

Race Car #12
Colgate-Palmolive
(Tidy Toy) 1960s
R – 4 $25.00 – 30.00
without box

Explosives Truck
Colgate-Palmolive
(Soaky Speed Toy) 1960s
R – 4 $25.00 – 30.00

Cement Truck
Colgate-Palmolive
(Soaky Speed Toy) 1960s
R – 4 $25.00 – 30.00

Oil Truck
Colgate-Palmolive
(Soaky Speed Toy) 1960s
R – 4 $25.00 – 30.00

Hot Wheels Race Car
Cosrich 1993
R – 2 $10.00 – 15.00

Matchbox Road Grader
Grosvenor (England) 1994
R – 3 $30.00 – 35.00

Custom Car
Avon
R – 4 $5.00 – 10.00

Dirt Movers Bulldozer
Prelude (England) 1995
R – 3 $20.00 – 25.00
In 1997, Minnetonka distributed an identical vehicle in both yellow and green and packaged in a box. Estimated value for vehicle and box is $5.00 – 10.00.

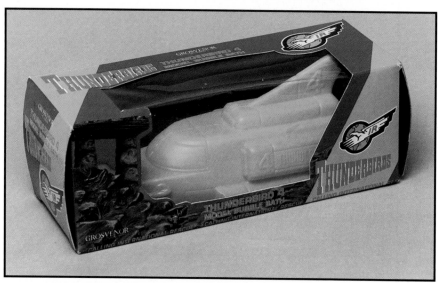

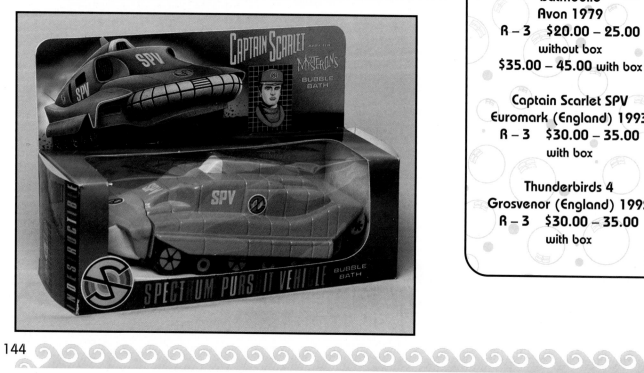

Batmobile — Batman Forever
Prelude (England) 1995
R – 3 $20.00 – 25.00

Batmobile
Avon 1979
R – 3 $20.00 – 25.00
without box
$35.00 – 45.00 with box

Captain Scarlet SPV
Euromark (England) 1993
R – 3 $30.00 – 35.00
with box

Thunderbirds 4
Grosvenor (England) 1992
R – 3 $30.00 – 35.00
with box

Stingray
Rosedew (England) 1993
R – 3 $20.00 – 25.00
with box

Space Precinct Police Cruiser
Euromark (England) 1995
R – 3 $25.00 – 30.00

Thunderbirds 2
Grosvenor (England) 1992
R – 3 $20.00 – 25.00
with box

Bubbly Boat (variation)
(Canada) 1986
R – 3 $10.00 – 15.00

Bubbly Boat (variation)
(Canada) 1986
R – 3 $10.00 – 15.00

Jungle Land Boat
Top Care (Canada) 1995
R – 3 $10.00 – 15.00

Jungle Land Boat
Top Care (Canada) 1995
R – 3 $10.00 – 15.00

Jungle Land Boat
Top Care (Canada) 1995
R – 3 $10.00 – 15.00

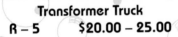

Transformer Truck
R – 5 $20.00 – 25.00

Transformer Truck Transformed

Game Boy Variations
Green: Grosvenor/IBN International 1997
Red: Cosmetic Import LTD 1997
Yellow: Grosvenor/IBN International 1997
R – 2 $5.00 – 10.00 each

Super Soaker • Cosrich 1992
R – 2 $10.00 – 15.00

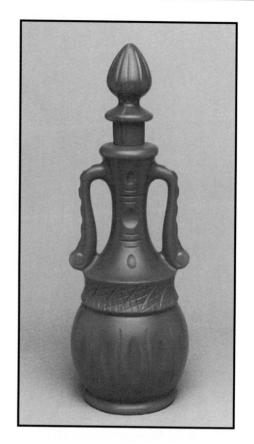

The Big Breakfast Teapot
Euromark (England) 1994
R – 3 $20.00 – 25.00

Genie Bottle
R – 4 $10.00 – 15.00

Pencil
R – 3 $5.00 – 10.00

Red Crayon
Penco 1993
R – 1 $2.00 – 5.00

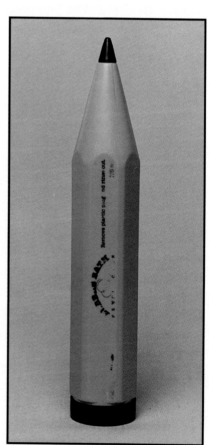

CHAPTER 12

•••● ● Avon ● ●•••

All estimated values in this chapter are for the bottle alone. For Avon bottles in the box, add $5.00.

Space Mission Decanter
Docking soap and
shampoo bottles
Avon 1988
R – 4 $10.00 – 15.00

Mr. Robottle
Avon 1972
R – 4 $10.00 – 15.00

Splash Down Space Capsule
Avon 1987
R – 3 $4.00 – 8.00

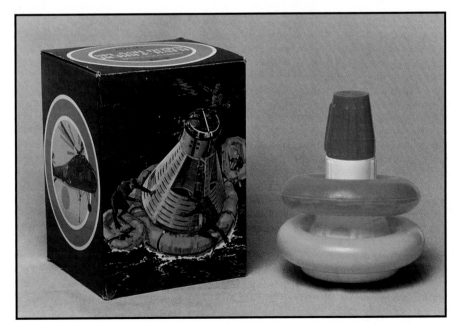

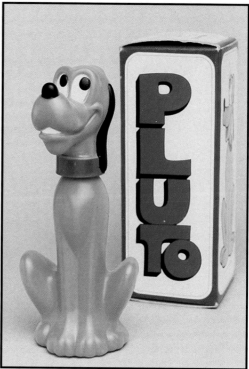

Aristocats
Avon 1971
R – 2 $4.00 – 8.00

Mickey Mouse
Avon 1970
R – 2 $4.00 – 8.00

Pluto
Avon 1970
R – 2 $4.00 – 8.00

Linus
Avon 1972
R – 2 $4.00 – 8.00

Schroeder (variation)
Avon 1970
R – 2 $4.00 – 8.00

Schroeder (variation) with piano
Avon 1970
R – 2 $15.00 – 20.00

Lucy • Avon 1972
R – 2 $5.00 – 10.00

Peanuts Pals • Avon 1972
R – 2 $5.00 – 10.00

Charlie Brown • Avon 1972
R – 2 $5.00 – 10.00

Snoopy the Flying Ace • Avon 1969
R – 2 $5.00 – 10.00

Snoopy on the Snow Flyer • Avon 1973
R – 3 $10.00 – 15.00

Snoopy's Ski Team • Avon 1975
R – 3 $15.00 – 20.00

Snoopy & Dog House • Avon 1969
R – 3 $5.00 – 10.00

Linus • Avon 1974
R – 3 $5.00 – 10.00

Snoopy's Bath Tub • Avon 1972
R – 3 $5.00 – 10.00

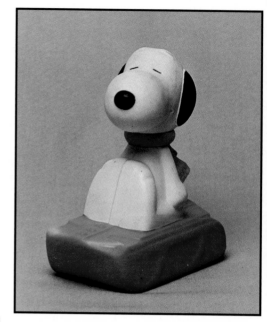

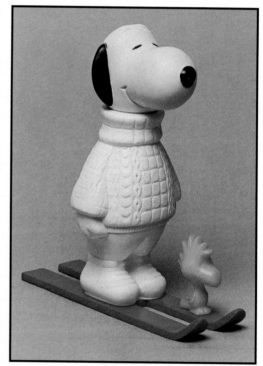

Charlie Brown Mug
Avon 1970
R – 3 $5.00 – 10.00

Snoopy Mug
Avon 1970
R – 3 $5.00 – 10.00

Lucy Mug
Avon 1970
R – 3 $5.00 – 10.00

Humpty Dumpty
Avon 1960s
R – 4 $5.00 – 10.00

Humpty Dumpty Takes a Fall

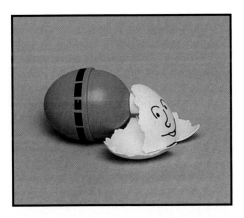

Santa's Chimney
Avon 1960s
R – 3 $5.00 – 10.00

Huggy Bear
Avon 1970s
R – 3 $5.00 – 10.00

Captain's Bubble Bath
Avon 1964
R – 4 $5.00 – 10.00

First Mate
Avon 1964
R – 4 $5.00 – 10.00

Most Valuable Gorilla
Avon 1980
R – 3 $5.00 – 10.00

Topsy Turvy Clown
Avon 1965
R – 4 $5.00 – 10.00

T - Rex
Avon
R – 3 $5.00 – 10.00

Triceratops
Avon
R – 3 $5.00 – 10.00

It's a Small World
Avon 1960s
R – 3 $5.00 – 10.00

It's a Small World
Avon 1960s
R – 3 $5.00 – 10.00

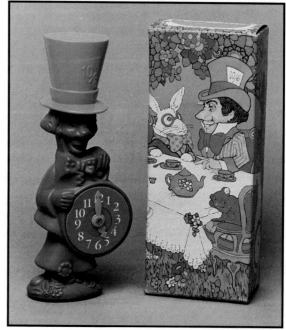

Freddy the Frog • Avon 1970s
R – 4 $5.00 – 10.00

Birdhouse • Avon 1969
R – 4 $5.00 – 10.00

Puffer Chugger • Avon 1972
R – 4 $5.00 – 10.00

Accusing Alligator • Avon 1979
R – 3 $5.00 – 10.00

Mouse Ran up the Clock • Avon 1972
R – 3 $5.00 – 10.00

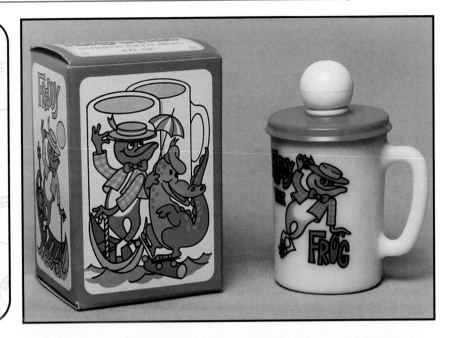

Name Game
Avon 1970s
R – 3 $5.00 – 10.00

Pop-a-Duck Game
Avon 1978
R – 4 $5.00 – 10.00

Li'l Folks Time
Avon 1964
R – 4 $5.00 – 10.00

Wabbit Car
Avon 1983
R – 4 $5.00 – 10.00

Whitey the Whale
Avon 1962
R – 4 $5.00 – 10.00

CHAPTER 13

·····●● Toppers ●●·····

Winnie the Pooh • Johnson & Johnson 1993
R – 1 $2.00 – 4.00

Piglet • Johnson & Johnson 1993
R – 1 $2.00 – 4.00

Tigger • Johnson & Johnson 1993
R – 1 $2.00 – 4.00

Eeyore • Johnson & Johnson 1993
R – 1 $2.00 – 4.00

Mickey Mouse • Johnson & Johnson 1996
R – 1 $2.00 – 4.00

Minnie Mouse • Johnson & Johnson 1996
R – 1 $2.00 – 4.00

Donald Duck • Johnson & Johnson 1996
R – 1 $2.00 – 4.00

Goofy • Johnson & Johnson 1996
R – 1 $2.00 – 4.00

Bart Simpson • Cosrich 1980s
R – 1 $15.00 – 20.00

Lisa Simpson • Cosrich 1980s
R – 1 $15.00 – 20.00

Homer Simpson • Cosrich 1980s
R – 1 $15.00 – 20.00

Marge Simpson • Cosrich 1980s
R – 1 $15.00 – 20.00

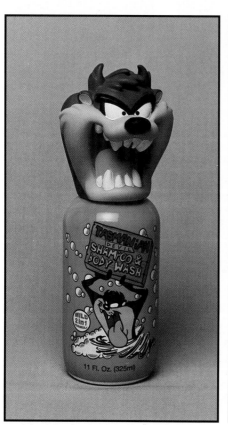

Sylvester
Minnetonka 1996
R – 1 $5.00 – 10.00

Tweety
Minnetonka 1996
R – 1 $5.00 – 10.00

Daffy Duck
Minnetonka 1996
R – 1 $5.00 – 10.00

Bugs Bunny
Minnetonka 1996
R – 1 $5.00 – 10.00

Tazmanian Devil
Minnetonka 1996
R – 1 $5.00 – 10.00

Bugs Bunny — Space Jam • Prelude (England) 1996
R – 1 $5.00 – 10.00

Daffy Duck — Space Jam • Prelude (England) 1996
R – 1 $5.00 – 10.00

Tazmanian Devil — Space Jam • Prelude (England) 1996
R – 1 $5.00 – 10.00

Wile E. Coyote — Space Jam • Prelude (England) 1996
R – 1 $5.00 – 10.00

Animaniacs
Ansehl 1995
R – 1
$5.00 – 10.00

Animaniacs
Ansehl 1995
R – 1
$5.00 – 10.00

Animaniacs
Ansehl 1995
R – 1
$5.00 – 10.00

Sonic the Hedgehog
Avon 1995
R – 2
$5.00 – 10.00

Princess Sally
Avon 1995
R – 2
$5.00 – 10.00

Knuckles
Avon 1995
R – 2
$5.00 – 10.00

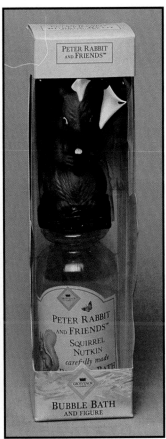

Peter Rabbit • Grosvenor (England) 1995
R – 2 $10.00 – 15.00

Benjamin Bunny • Grosvenor (England) 1995
R – 2 $10.00 – 15.00

Tom Kitten • Grosvenor (England) 1995
R – 2 $10.00 – 15.00

Squirrel Nutkin • Grosvenor (England) 1995
R – 2 $10.00 – 15.00

Mrs. Tiggy Winkle • Grosvenor (England) 1995
R – 2 $10.00 – 15.00

Jemima Puddle Duck • Grosvenor (England) 1995
R – 2 $10.00 – 15.00

Spider-man
Kid Care 1995
R – 1 $5.00 – 10.00

Power Ranger
Kid Care 1995
R – 1 $5.00 – 10.00

Black Power Ranger
Avon 1995
R – 2 $5.00 – 10.00

Blue Power Ranger
Avon 1995
R – 2 $5.00 – 10.00

Red Power Ranger
Avon 1995
R – 2 $5.00 – 10.00

Batman
Kid Care 1991
R – 2 $5.00 – 10.00

Michelangelo — Ninja Turtle
Kid Care 1989
R – 2 $10.00 – 15.00

Shreader
Kid Care 1989
R – 2 $10.00 – 15.00

Megazord
Kid Care 1995
R – 1 $1.00 – 5.00

Little Mermaid
Kid Care 1991
R – 2 $10.00 – 15.00

Beast
Centura (Canada) 1995
R – 1 $5.00 – 10.00

The Hunchback of Notre Dame
Kid Care 1996
R – 1 $5.00 – 10.00

Esmeralda
Kid Care 1996
R – 1 $5.00 – 10.00

The Lion King
Centura (Canada) 1995
R – 3 $10.00 – 15.00

Nala
Centura (Canada) 1995
R – 3 $10.00 – 15.00

Pumbaa
Centura (Canada) 1995
R – 3 $10.00 – 15.00

Operation Aliens
Grosvenor (England) 1993
R – 3 $25.00 – 30.00

First Contact — Star Trek
1996
R – 1 $4.00 – 8.00

Ghostbusters Ectoplasm
R – 3 $10.00 – 15.00

Rupert
M. Hall (England) 1995
R – 3 $25.00 – 30.00

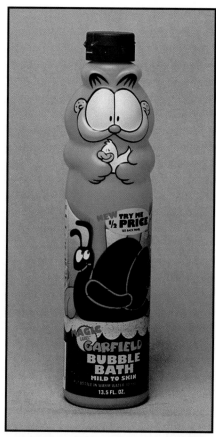

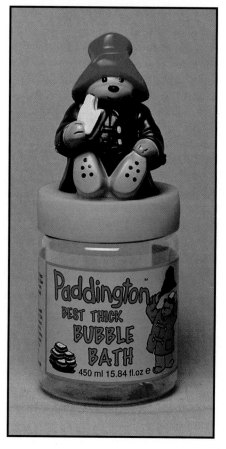

Barbie
Grosvenor (England) 1996
R – 3 $15.00 – 20.00

Garfield
Johnson & Johnson 1994
R – 1 $1.00 – 5.00

Where's Waldo
Cosrich 1989
R – 2 $15.00 – 20.00

Paddington Bear
Cottsmore (England) 1990s
R – 3 $20.00 – 25.00

Mad Balls
DuCair Bioescence 1986
R – 2 $15.00 – 20.00

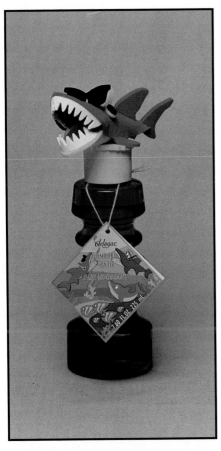

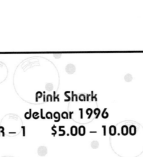

Pink Shark
deLagar 1996
R – 1 $5.00 – 10.00

Blue Shark
deLagar 1996
R – 1 $5.00 – 10.00

Fish
deLagar 1996
R – 1 $5.00 – 10.00

Pink Dolphin
deLagar 1996
R – 1 $5.00 – 10.00

Dolphin's Football
Cosrich 1992
R – 2 $5.00 – 10.00

Raider's Football
Cosrich 1992
R – 2 $5.00 – 10.00

Oiler's Football
Cosrich 1992
R – 2 $5.00 – 10.00

Bronco's Football
Cosrich 1992
R – 2 $5.00 – 10.00

Eagle's Football
Cosrich 1992
R – 2 $5.00 – 10.00

Giant's Football
Cosrich 1992
R – 2 $5.00 – 10.00

Cowboy's Football
Cosrich 1992
R – 2 $5.00 – 10.00

Redskin's Football
Cosrich 1992
R – 2 $5.00 – 10.00

Packer's Football
Cosrich 1992
R – 2 $5.00 – 10.00

Viking's Football
Cosrich 1992
R – 2 $5.00 – 10.00

Bear's Football
Cosrich 1992
R – 2 $5.00 – 10.00

Lion's Football
Cosrich 1992
R – 2 $5.00 – 10.00

49er's Football
Cosrich 1992
R – 2 $5.00 – 10.00

INDEX

COLLECTOR BOOKS

A Division of Schroeder Publishing Co., Inc.

ISBN 1-57432-074-2

9 781574 320749

US$19.95